Danube River Cruise Travel Guide 2024

The Most Update & Essential Guide For New Visitors To Explore Danube's Landscape With Map & Images,Itinerary,Cuisine, Top Attractions,Hotels,Culture & Historical Adventure.

Betty Caulfield

Table of Contents

Introduction: Unveiling the Danube's Enchantment

Embarking on a trek down the serpentine ribbon of the Danube, I found myself immersed in a narrative of liquid history and cultural resonance. The river, like a serpentine storyteller, runs through the heart of Europe, revealing mysteries of civilizations long ago.

As I glanced at the Danube's glassy surface, I couldn't help but sense the weight of its tale. My expedition started when the river flirted with the German Black Forest, and as I followed its route, I marveled at the confluence of waterways that had seen the rise and fall of civilizations.

The Danube isn't only a river; it's an articulate poet, carving poems in the shape of valleys, meanders, and bends. With each passing kilometer, I floated past pages of history, a living tapestry fashioned by the hands of time.

Navigating its currents, I met the ruins of old civilizations, as if the river itself were an archeological guide. Roman ruins arose on its banks, standing stoically against the currents of change. The medieval whispers of knights and troubadours lingered in the air as we floated by magnificent castles that once guarded trade routes and legacies.

Yet, the Danube isn't a static museum. It vibrates with life, a lively canvas created by the civilizations along its coasts. In places where time appeared to pause, inhabitants recounted their experiences over substantial meals, delivering a flavor of the region's culinary legacy that dances on the taste senses.

The river's embrace stretched beyond the physical; it caressed the invisible soul of the countries it traversed. As I sailed, I felt a link with the essence of Central Europe, with the echoes of tunes from magnificent concert halls and the laughter ringing from riverbank cafés.

In the golden glory of dusk, the Danube unveiled its charm, weaving a spell that surpassed the boundaries of a normal travelog. It became a tour of self-discovery, a flowing adventure that matched the ever-changing scenery along its banks.

So, to explore the Danube is to begin on a personal symphony, where the river's sounds echo with the pulse of Europe's history, present, and the possibilities of travels still to unfold.

Purpose of the Guide

Navigating the Danube's Rich Tapestry.

This book is more than a compendium of itineraries and practical recommendations; it's a compass for accessing the essence of a Danube River trip. Its objective goes beyond navigation, seeking to convert your trip into an engaging exploration of history, culture, and remarkable encounters.

As you begin your excursion, the guide acts as a knowledgeable companion, giving insights into the Danube's cultural tapestry. It tries to link you with the pulse of the river, diving into the historical depths that have influenced the landscapes and communities along its borders.

Beyond technical information, the book attempts to evoke a feeling of wanderlust, urging you to not only observe but to connect with the colorful tales woven into the fabric of the Danube. It seeks to divert your focus beyond the stunning vistas, urging you to explore the intricacies of each site, from hidden jewels to recognizable monuments.

Practicality meets enthusiasm as the guide handles the subtleties of planning, from picking the proper cruise to relishing local food. It aims to provide you with the knowledge to navigate the waters of the Danube confidently, ensuring that every curve in the river becomes a chance for exploration.

In essence, the objective of this book is to transform your Danube River trip from a normal holiday to an engaging voyage. It encourages you to immerse yourself in the cultural symphony resonating along the riverbanks, forging a relationship with the legacy, people, and landscapes that make the Danube a timeless wonder.

Chapter 2. Understanding the Danube

Exploring the Danube's Geographical Tapestry.

The Danube, a beautiful thread running through the heart of Europe, creates a geographical tale that emerges with every bend and turn. Originating in the Black Forest of Germany, this legendary river goes on a voyage that spans a broad spectrum of landscapes, guaranteeing a visual feast for the enthusiastic visitor.

As the Danube weaves its way through the Bavarian countryside, gorgeous hills and valleys cradle its banks, producing a serene view that contrasts with the lively energy of adjacent towns. Moving southeast, the river becomes a natural boundary, slicing through the Austrian Alps with astonishing precision, presenting panoramic vistas that fascinate both the sight and the mind.

The adventure continues as the Danube meanders into the center of Vienna, where the urban environment harmoniously mixes with the river's flow. From the magnificent bridges that cross its waters to the architectural treasures bordering the banks, the Danube becomes a living painting reflecting the cultural grandeur of the towns it encompasses.

Further downstream, the river meets the Hungarian plains, a wide expanse that spreads in rhythmic accord with the meadows and vineyards dotting the landscape. The Danube's rivers bring with them a feeling of continuity, uniting the different terrains it meets, from the undulating hills of Germany to the flat plains of Hungary.

The river's voyage concludes at the Danube Delta, a UNESCO World Heritage Site where its waters dance with the Black Sea. Here, a network of channels and marshes forms a unique ecology, showing nature's beauty at the river's ultimate destination.

In essence, the Danube's geographical characteristics are a living tableau, a tribute to the river's power to change and be influenced by the landscapes it adorns. As you begin on your trip, each length of the Danube exposes a new chapter in its geological tale, enabling you to experience the magnificence of a river that feeds life into the heart of Europe.

Tracing the Historical Epic of the Danube

The Danube River, a liquid record carved across the European continent, rushes not just with water but with the whispers of history. Its banks have borne witness to the rise and fall of empires, the footsteps of invaders, and the echoes of ancient civilizations.

The narrative starts in the Roman Empire when the Danube served as a natural boundary of the empire, a liquid protection against invading troops. The relics of Roman forts and archeological riches surrounding the riverbanks serve as palpable reflections of this bygone age when the Danube was more than a waterway; it was a boundary of power and influence.

As the medieval ages developed, the Danube became an important commerce route, linking civilizations and supporting economic prosperity. Mighty strongholds and castles, placed strategically along its stream, relate tales of territorial struggles and the strategic necessity of controlling the river's flow.

The Renaissance and Baroque eras brought a flowering of art and culture to the Danube's banks. Magnificent palaces and enormous cathedrals, each with its narrative of creative genius, remain evidence of an age when the river became a conduit for the interchange of ideas and creativity.

The Danube, however, did not only observe history; it played a key part in molding it. The Ottoman Empire's growth was characterized by wars along the river's banks, leaving behind a legacy of cultural fusion that pervades the area to this day.

In the 20th century, the Danube found itself at the crossroads of geopolitical upheavals. From the Cold War period, when it functioned as a natural boundary between East and West, until the collapse of the Iron

Curtain, the river's currents paralleled the ebb and flow of political tides.

Today, when you ride down the Danube, each curve in the river uncovers layers of history. The cities and villages that have evolved along its banks carry the footprints of centuries past, affording a physical link to the historical fabric that makes the Danube not simply a river but a living monument to Europe's rich and complicated history.

Diverse Cultural Influences: Danube's Living Mosaic

The Danube River, with its serpentine route across Central Europe, acts as a cultural kaleidoscope, reflecting the bright colors of the different cultures that have developed along its banks. As you begin on a voyage down this liquid roadway, you'll find yourself immersed in a living tapestry of traditions, art, and rituals.

The Germanic legacy that embraces the river's beginnings in the Black Forest sets the scene for the cultural symphony that follows. Timber-framed towns and the echoes of German folklore create an aura that testifies to a rich past anchored in the heart of Europe.

Moving southeast into Austria, the Danube smoothly waltzes past Vienna, a city famous for classical music, art, and imperial splendor. The Habsburg past is evident, reflected in the sumptuous palaces, exquisite architecture, and the very air that echoes with the tunes of Mozart and Strauss.

As the river runs into Hungary, a unique combination of Magyar traditions and Turkish influences develops. Budapest, with its hot spas, Ottoman-era buildings, and busy marketplaces, highlights the cultural crossroads where East meets West along the Danube's meandering path.

The Danube doesn't only absorb culture; it produces it. The riverbanks are dotted with picturesque towns where local artists produce traditional items, and folk festivals commemorate age-old traditions. Each port of call becomes a stage where regional dances, music, and gastronomic delicacies take the center limelight, enabling passengers to engage in the vibrant culture of the Danube.

Serbia and Bulgaria lend their chapters to this cultural tale, as Orthodox monasteries, traditional music, and local handicrafts add layers to the Danube's developing character. The river becomes a uniting factor, linking communities while allowing their originality to show.

In essence, the Danube is not a passive witness to culture; it's a dynamic force that develops a feeling of unity among variety.

As you cruise along its currents, you'll find yourself immersed in a continual conversation of civilizations, each contributing to the harmonic tune that characterizes the cultural symphony of the Danube.

Chapter 3. Planning Your Danube River Cruise

Navigating the Danube: Choosing the Right Cruise

In the search to pick the ideal Danube River trip, I learned that the adventure starts long before stepping foot on the ship. It's a delicate ballet of factors that mixes personal tastes, travel style, and the draw of locations along the way.

1. Define Your Priorities: When I began on my Danube trip, I first decided what mattered most to me. Was it the cultural immersion in historic cities, the gorgeous landscapes, or possibly the gastronomic experiences? Knowing my criteria helped limit the variety of cruise alternatives accessible.

2. Cruise Duration & Itinerary: The Danube provides a tapestry of locations, each with its distinct beauty. I assessed how much time I wanted to commit to the travel and the particular cities or places I intended to investigate. Some cruises concentrate on a single location, while others explore the full length of the river.

3. Cruise Style: River cruises come in numerous forms, from tiny boutique boats to bigger ships with greater facilities. Reflecting on my own tastes, I decided on a mid-sized cruise that provided a combination of comfort and customized encounters. It was like discovering a floating house that matched my travel style.

4. Time of Year: The seasons have a crucial part in establishing the Danube experience. Spring and summer give colorful vistas, while autumn delivers a tapestry of warm hues. Winter cruises capture the enchantment of festive marketplaces. Considering the time of year was essential in establishing the vibe I intended.

5. Cruise Lines and Reviews: Research became my valued companion. Reading reviews, comparing facilities, and learning the reputation of various cruise companies enabled me to make an educated selection. I wanted a cruise business that resonated with my standards for service and genuineness.

In the end, I picked a midsummer trip that promised a combination of cultural exploration and visual wonders. The ship, endowed with panoramic windows, became my floating vantage point for fascinating landscapes and ancient towns. From eating local foods on board to partaking in guided tours that brought history to life, every element coincided with the customized experience I desired.

Choosing the correct Danube River trip became a vital component of structuring my vacation. It was more than a practical choice; it was an intentional move towards constructing an experience that corresponded with my travel objectives, making the Danube a liquid canvas upon which my voyage evolved.

Planning your Danube River cruise involves a deliberate assessment of the optimum times to set sail, guaranteeing a balanced combination of excellent weather, cultural celebrations, and visual splendor.

1. Spring Splendor (April to June): As the Danube wakes from winter's embrace, spring sends a rush of color to the riverbanks. Cruising during this season enables you to observe flowering sceneries, mild temperatures, and fewer tourists. It's a wonderful season for nature lovers and those wanting a more serene experience.

2. Summer Serenity (July to August): The summer months provide a particular appeal with longer days and a bustling ambiance. Cruise beneath the warm sun, discovering vibrant cities and enjoying outdoor activities. Be careful of increasing visitor traffic and consider arranging trips in advance to reserve your space.

3. Autumn Awe (September to October): As the leaves change hues, autumn illuminates the Danube with a spectrum of warm colors. The weather stays favorable, and the harvest season brings a new gastronomic experience. This time offers a balance between visual splendor and pleasant sailing conditions.

4. Winter Wonder (November to March): While less popular for sailing, the winter months lend a calm

beauty to the Danube. If you're attracted to beautiful Christmas markets and don't mind lower temps, a winter cruise might be a fantastic experience. Just be prepared for intermittent closures and restricted outside activity.

Consider your tastes and goals when picking the schedule of your Danube River trip. Whether it's the bloom of spring, the warmth of summer, the bright hues of autumn, or the magic of winter, each season along the Danube uncovers a separate chapter of its fascination.

Duration and Itinerary Considerations

Crafting Your Danube Odyssey.

Embarking on a Danube River cruise is an invitation to a trip through history, culture, and visual splendor. As you design your vacation, the length of your cruise and the carefully crafted itinerary will influence the depth of your experience.

Danube Sampler: 7-Day Exploration

- For those with limited time, a week-long voyage delivers a tantalizing sample of the Danube's delights. Setting out from Passau, Germany, and culminating in Budapest, Hungary, this itinerary brings you to important features. Marvel at the baroque splendors of Melk Abbey, wander through Vienna's imperial gardens, and experience the hot spas in Budapest. While the ride is quick, it's a fantastic introduction to the cultural and architectural gems along the river.

The Grand Danube Expedition: 14-Day Immersion

- For a more thorough experience, a two-week trip provides for a deeper investigation of the Danube's various landscapes and historical tapestry. Beginning in Nuremberg, Germany, and concluding in the Black Sea, this lengthy voyage spans the famed towns of Vienna and Budapest but also delves into lesser-known treasures like Bratislava and Belgrade. With additional days incorporated into the schedule, you may indulge in unhurried excursions, unearthing hidden gems and developing relationships with the local culture.

Enchanting Danube Seasons: Tailored Four-Season Cruises

- Consider the lovely dance of the Danube over the seasons. A spring cruise may feature flowering riverfront scenery, while a summer excursion bathes you in bright sunshine for outdoor adventures. Fall delivers a tapestry of seasonal hues, while a winter cruise uncovers a new type of charm with Christmas marketplaces. Tailor your length and itinerary to reflect the seasonal charm that resonates best with your travel tastes.

Whichever length and itinerary you pick, the Danube provides a symphony of sensations. Whether it's a fast overture or a long work, your river trip is a chance to immerse yourself in the fascinating melodies of Europe's cultural core.

7-Day Danube Exploration: A Symphony of Highlights

Day 1-2: Passau, Germany
- Embark on your tour at Passau, where the Danube, Inn, and Ilz rivers confluence.

- Explore the picturesque Old Town, noted for its baroque architecture.
- Visit St. Stephen's Cathedral and the magnificent Veste Oberhaus castle.

Day 3: Linz, Austria
- Cruise to Linz, a city with a thriving arts and cultural scene.
- Discover the Ars Electronica Center and indulge in Linzer Torte, a local specialty.
- Optional trip to the historic village of Český Krumlov over the Czech border.

Day 4: Melk & Dürnstein
- Sail to Melk and explore the spectacular Melk Abbey, a UNESCO World Heritage site.
- Continue to Dürnstein, a lovely village with a castle and cobblestone streets.
- Enjoy a wine-tasting adventure in the Wachau Valley.

Day 5-6: Vienna, Austria
- Arrive in Vienna, the city of classical music and imperial magnificence.
- Explore the Schönbrunn Palace, St. Stephen's Cathedral, and the Belvedere Palace.
- Attend a classical concert or opera for a true Viennese experience.

Day 7: Budapest, Hungary

- Conclude your adventure in Budapest, a city split by the Danube.
- Visit Buda Castle, Fisherman's Bastion, and bathe in the warm baths.
- Optional nighttime cruise for panoramic views of Budapest's lit monuments.

14-Day Danube Immersion: Unveiling Hidden Treasures

Day 1-3: Nuremberg, Germany
- Start your long voyage at Nuremberg, noted for its medieval architecture.
- Explore the ancient Old Town, Nuremberg Castle, and the Documentation Center.
- Visit the Nazi Party Rally Grounds and Courtroom 600, location of the Nuremberg Trials.

Day 4-5: Regensburg & Passau
- Cruise to Regensburg, a UNESCO World Heritage city with well-preserved medieval architecture.
- Continue to Passau, experiencing its baroque grandeur and enjoying a magnificent riverbank stroll.

Day 6: Linz, Austria
- Spend a day in Linz, diving deeper into its cultural offers.
- Visit the Lentos Art Museum and the Brucknerhaus performance venue.

Day 7: Dürnstein & Melk
- Return to Dürnstein for a more leisurely investigation of its vineyards and history.
- Revisit Melk Abbey for an in-depth tour, enjoying its art and architecture.

Day 8-9: Vienna, Austria
- Enjoy a prolonged stay in Vienna, allowing for greater cultural immersion.
- Explore lesser-known areas, explore small markets, and sample real Viennese food.

Day 10-11: Bratislava, Slovakia
- Cruise to Bratislava, a city steeped in history and beauty.
- Visit Bratislava Castle, meander through the Old Town, and enjoy Slovakian delights.

Day 12-14: Budapest, Hungary
- Conclude your immersive experience in Budapest.
- Explore off-the-beaten-path areas, visit the Hungarian National Museum, and indulge in local food.

- Spend your last day with a soothing spa session and a farewell meal overlooking the Danube.

Scenic Views and Natural Wonders

Cruising down the Danube is not simply a tour through history and culture; it's a visual feast of beautiful landscapes and natural beauties that sear themselves into memory. As the river meanders over varied terrains, every bend unveils a new chapter in the tale of Europe's natural splendor.

One of the most fascinating elements is the Wachau Valley, where the river is hugged by undulating hills covered in vineyards and sprinkled with picturesque towns. The vine-clad hills form a patchwork quilt of greenery, and the ancient villages like Dürnstein look like time capsules tucked against this beautiful background. I recall standing on the terrace, watching the sun shed a golden light over the valley, and feeling as if I had walked into a picture.

Cruising over the Austrian Alps, the view morphs into a breathtaking symphony of peaks and valleys. The cool mountain air, the snow-capped peaks, and the mirror-like reflections on the river created a tranquil mood. It was a moment of absolute peace, a contact with nature's majesty that left an unforgettable impact on my spirit.

As we traversed the Danube Delta towards the Black Sea, the scenery took a dramatic transformation. The delta is a dynamic tapestry of canals, marshes, and reed beds alive with animals. Flocks of birds flew above, and the rustling reeds made a relaxing song. Exploring this unusual habitat was like entering a place undisturbed by time, where nature determined the cycle of existence.

An unexpected pleasure was the Iron Gates, a tiny valley between Serbia and Romania. The towering cliffs, formed by the river over millennia, evoked a feeling of awe. The trip through this natural treasure seemed like a cinematic odyssey, with every twist and turn exposing new layers of the raw beauty that lined the Danube.

These encounters underlined the Danube's function as a conduit not merely for human history but for the forces that formed the country itself. The picturesque vistas and natural marvels along the river are not simply things to see; they are moments of connection with the Earth's beauty, reminders of the delicate dance between water and land that has played out over millennia along the Danube's meandering journey.

Unique Flora and Fauna

The Danube River, frequently acclaimed for its cultural and historical tapestry, also uncovers a rich canvas of distinct flora and wildlife along its banks. During my own Danube River trip, the meeting with this unique ecology gave an unexpected depth of enchantment to the voyage.

Flora: A Riverside Symphony

As the ship drifted into the Wachau Valley, the hillsides came alive with a colorful display of flowers. Vineyards cascaded down the hills, their leaves catching the sunshine in shades of green and gold. Wildflowers lined the riverbanks, producing a kaleidoscope of hues that swirled in the air. Orchards of apricot and apple trees provided their smell to the air, enriching the sensory pleasure of the ride.

One especially memorable occasion was a guided nature walk in Austria when our group explored a riverbank route. The guide showed us native flora, describing their medical applications and cultural value. We discovered delicate wild orchids and the powerful blooms of alpine meadowfoam, each adding to the ecological symphony that matched the flow of the Danube.

Another highlight was a tour across the Danube Delta, where the river pours into the Black Sea. Here, the wetlands explode with life, presenting a rich assortment of aquatic plants, reeds, and water lilies. It was like walking into a watercolor painting, with each stroke of nature's brush producing a masterpiece of biodiversity.

Fauna: Wildlife Along the Banks

As the journey proceeded, the Danube disclosed its secret dwellers. Birds of prey swooped above, their sharp eyes seeking for fish in the river. Swans flew effortlessly down the river, while ducks and herons took safety in quiet nooks. The banks resonated with the sounds of songbirds, providing a natural soundtrack that accompanied our trek.

One morning, while on a beach trip in the Danube Delta, our little boat cruised through tight passages and reed-lined streams. It was here that we met the varied bird community that makes the delta home. From beautiful egrets to bright kingfishers, the trip was a birdwatcher's heaven.

In the middle of majestic castles and old towns, the presence of the Danube's vegetation and animals afforded moments of calm relaxation. One evening, as the sun fell below the horizon, I found myself on the ship's deck, watching a family of swans fly past. It was a simple but meaningful moment, a reminder that within the human tale, the river's environment maintained its ageless dance.

In essence, the distinctive flora and wildlife along the Danube gave a layer of natural poetry to the cultural and historical epic of the river. It served as a reminder that, behind the architectural wonders and legendary towns, the Danube is a real, breathing organism with its own tale to tell—one written in the language of leaves, flowers, and the soft rustling of riverside reeds.

Outdoor Activities near the Riverbanks

Hiking in the Scenic Wachau Valley: A Nature Lover's Paradise

The Wachau Valley, lying along the banks of the Danube between Melk and Krems in Austria, welcomes hikers with its stunning vistas and lovely vineyards. Embarking on a hiking expedition in the Wachau Valley is a voyage into a world where terraced vines, ancient castles, and lovely towns unfold like chapters in a novel.

Key Highlights:

1. Dürnstein to Krems Trail:
   - Start your tour at the medieval village of Dürnstein, noted for its castle remains and historic beauty.
   - Hike along well-marked paths that lead to Krems, affording beautiful views of the Danube and the adjacent vine-covered hills.
   - Pass past apricot orchards and small wine towns, immersing yourself in the region's agricultural riches.

2. Vineyard Panoramas:
   - Traverse terraced vineyards that carpet the hillsides, creating a visual feast of neat rows of grapevines against the background of the river.
   - Visit local vineyards along the road, where you may indulge in wine tastings and learn about the traditional winemaking practices.

3. Ruins of Castle Dürnstein:
   - Take a detour to visit the remains of Castle Dürnstein, positioned high above the town.
   - Enjoy panoramic views of the Danube Valley from the castle's high point, giving an ideal site for a break and contemplation.

4. Krems Old Town Exploration:
  - Conclude your journey at Krems, a town with a well-preserved medieval old town.
  - Wander through cobblestone streets, uncover old houses, and relax at one of the local cafés to taste the distinct ambiance.

Tips for Hikers:

  - Trail Difficulty: The hiking routes in the Wachau Valley appeal to varied fitness levels. Choose paths that fit your hiking expertise and endurance.
  - Seasonal Considerations: Spring and fall bring pleasant temperatures and beautiful sceneries. Summer might be warmer, great for individuals who appreciate longer daylight hours. Winter treks are feasible, although trail conditions may vary.

  - Appropriate Footwear: Wear strong hiking shoes, particularly if exploring dirt routes in vineyards or mountainous terrain.

Hiking in the Wachau Valley is more than a physical adventure; it's an immersive experience that enables you to connect with the natural beauty and cultural richness of this famous Austrian area.

Kayaking or canoeing on the Danube gives a unique and personal view of this renowned river, enabling fans to immerse themselves in its natural beauty and cultural richness. Here's a taste of the experience:

1. Tranquil Waters & Scenic Beauty:
   - Paddling along the Danube gives a pleasant and peaceful experience as you negotiate its calm waters.
   - The riverbanks expand with stunning views, with wineries, small towns, and lush flora.

2. Flexibility of Exploration:
   - Kayaking or canoeing offers you freedom in exploration, allowing you to explore isolated regions and secret coves that may be off the usual road.
   - Navigate at your own speed, deciding whether to float along lazily or crank up the pace for a touch of thrill.

3. Close Encounters with Nature:
   - Glide silently across the water, allowing you the chance for intimate encounters with the rich animals along the riverbanks.
   - Birdwatching becomes a thrill as you view herons, swans, and other waterfowl in their natural environment.

4. Historical and Cultural Perspectives:

- Many historical sights and landmarks are located along the Danube, and kayaking or canoeing allows a unique aspect to admire these structures from the river.
- Paddle past historic castles, riverfront strongholds, and picturesque towns that tell stories of years past.

5. Adventure and Relaxation Combined:
- While the Danube provides a serene kayaking experience, there are also portions with modest rapids for those wanting a touch of action.
- Enjoy the blend of energetic exploration and the calm of floating with the currents.

6. Multi-Day Expeditions:
- For the brave at heart, multi-day kayaking or canoeing adventures are offered, enabling you to travel greater portions of the Danube and enjoy its different landscapes.
- Camping along the riverbanks beneath the starlit sky adds an element of adventure to the excursion.

7. Local Guided Tours:
- Local outfitters typically provide guided kayaking or canoeing trips, giving insights into the region's history, culture, and environment.
- Experienced guides may improve your trip by sharing anecdotes and pointing out hidden treasures along the route.

Kayaking or canoeing on the Danube isn't simply a physical sport; it's a complete experience that integrates natural adventure with cultural inquiry, delivering a unique view of this ancient and lovely river.

Birdwatching along the Danube Riverbanks is a thrilling experience, enabling lovers to witness numerous bird species in their natural settings. From the beautiful glide of swans to the nimble movements of herons and cormorants, the riverbanks serve as a sanctuary for numerous species. During a leisurely walk or sail, one may watch these winged dwellers, adding to the natural charm of the area. Birdwatchers may also meet migratory species, adding an element of seasonal richness to the avian display along the Danube.

Especially remarkable is the presence of songbirds, filling the air with lovely tunes as they flutter among the trees and reeds. Riverside towns and natural reserves along the Danube provide perfect vantage points for birding, giving a calm atmosphere where enthusiasts may view, identify, and enjoy the varied wildlife. The different habitats along the riverbanks create a dynamic atmosphere, making birding a satisfying and quiet outdoor activity for anyone seeking a connection with nature during their Danube River voyage.

Golfing with Panoramic River Views

Golf aficionados may enjoy a unique and gorgeous experience along the Danube, where the tranquil beauty of the riverbanks forms the background for a game of golf. Imagine teeing off against the lush greens with the gorgeous river flowing in the background, creating a backdrop that mixes the accuracy of the sport with the peacefulness of nature.

Several golf courses along the Danube provide not only tough fairways but also stunning views of the river and adjacent scenery. These courses, intentionally constructed to make the most of the natural topography, give golfers an immersive experience that extends beyond the game itself.

As you swing through your round, the rhythmic flow of the Danube acts as a pleasant background. The courses typically blend the curves of the terrain, offering vantage spots that enable players to stop, take in the view, and enjoy the particular appeal of playing among such natural beauty.

From the fairways, you could get sights of riverfront towns, historic sites, and, depending on the time of day, the shifting hues of the sky reflected in the water. Whether you're a seasoned golfer or a casual player, the mix of sport and landscape along the Danube adds a layer of calm and delight to the golfing experience.

It's not simply a game of accuracy and skill; it's a chance to immerse yourself in the visual beauty of the Danube, where every swing becomes a part of the greater symphony that the river leads across the landscapes it adorns.

Engaging in yoga or meditation by the Danube River is a calm and refreshing experience that harmonizes the relaxing natural surroundings with focused activities. Here, the steady flow of the river and the calm scenery make a great backdrop for people seeking moments of inner peace and introspection.

1. Riverside Yoga Sessions:
   - Yoga by the Danube frequently includes putting up mats or practicing on grassy riverbanks.
   - The rhythmic sounds of the rushing water create a peaceful soundtrack to yoga positions and stretches.
   - Instructors lead participants through positions, developing a connection with nature and self.

2. Meditation Amidst Nature:
   - Finding a peaceful location by the river, people may participate in meditation to the calming symphony of nature.
   - The mild wind, the murmur of water, and the rustling of leaves create a peaceful mood.
   - Practitioners frequently concentrate on mindfulness, breathing, and grounding practices, connecting with the present moment.

3. Sunrise or Sunset Sessions:

- Many opt to practice yoga or meditation during the lovely moments of dawn or sunset.
- The delicate colors painting the sky and the reflection on the lake enhance the experience, providing a serene mood.
- This gives a nice start or finish to the day, generating a feeling of balance and thankfulness.

4. Group Retreats and Workshops:
- Some sites along the Danube host group yoga retreats or courses, combining practice with wellness activities.
- Experienced teachers take participants through programs that include both physical postures and emotional well-being.

5. Connection with Nature:
- Practicing yoga or meditation by the river helps folks to bond with nature and find consolation in the simplicity of the setting.
- The openness of the riverbanks and the broad vistas add to a feeling of spaciousness and peace.

6. Accessible to All Levels:
- Whether a seasoned practitioner or a novice, yoga or meditation by the Danube is accessible to all levels of expertise.
- The natural environment enables individuals to go at their own speed, establishing a non-competitive and welcoming attitude.

In essence, yoga or meditation by the Danube delivers a comprehensive experience, mixing the advantages of awareness with the restorative impacts of nature. It's a chance to cultivate the body, mind, and spirit in an environment that perfectly integrates the beauty of the river with the desire of inner peace.

Fishing for Local Species Along the Danube

Fishing along the Danube provides not simply a leisure pastime but an opportunity to connect with the river's rich aquatic ecosystem. Whether you're an expert fisherman or a beginner, the Danube's waters offer an inviting atmosphere to cast your line and engage with the local fishing culture.

Key Aspects:

1. Diverse Fish Species:
   - The Danube is home to a broad variety of fish species, including carp, catfish, perch, pike, and more.
   - Anglers have the ability to target certain species based on the area and time of year.

2. Scenic Fishing Spots:
   - Riverside towns and villages frequently have dedicated fishing locations, creating a scenic background for fishermen.

- Tranquil backwaters and meandering lengths create excellent circumstances for a peaceful fishing experience.

3. Local Fishing Culture:
   - Engaging with local fishermen and fishing communities gives a cultural dimension to the experience.
   - Learning about traditional fishing tactics and techniques may increase your respect for the region's history.

4. Catch-and-Release Practices:
   - Many regions along the Danube encourage catch-and-release procedures to conserve the ecology.
   - Understanding local legislation encourages proper fishing and supports conservation efforts.

5. Guided Fishing Excursions:
   - Opting for guided fishing expeditions led by local experts increases the entire experience.
   - Guides not only give vital insights into the greatest fishing areas but also tell tales about the river's history and the importance of various fish species.

6. Seasonal Variations:
   - Fishing circumstances fluctuate with the seasons, impacting the behavior of fish.

- Spring and early summer may be excellent seasons for particular species, while fall provides various options.

7. Equipment and Techniques:
- Tailor your fishing gear to the precise species you're targeting.
- From fly fishing for trout to utilizing bait for catfish, changing your approach boosts the probability of a good catch.

8. Relaxation and Connection:
- Fishing beside the Danube gives a calm and thoughtful experience.
- Whether it's a solitary attempt or a shared pastime with companions, it gives a unique opportunity to interact with the natural beauty of the river.

Remember to verify local legislation, get any required permissions, and maintain sustainable fishing techniques to preserve a happy cohabitation with the Danube's aquatic ecology.

Horseback Riding Near River Towns

An Equestrian Adventure

Immerse yourself in the magnificent sceneries along the Danube by enjoying horseback riding among the charming river villages. This outdoor sport gives a fresh viewpoint, enabling you to cross gorgeous routes, enjoy the peacefulness of the countryside, and observe the splendor of the Danube from a different vantage point.

Key Experiences:

1. Riverside pathways: Explore meandering pathways that run through river villages, affording vistas of exquisite architecture, lush meadows, and the peaceful flow of the Danube.

2. Countryside Exploration: Venture into the surrounding countryside, uncovering hidden jewels that may be unavailable by other methods. Horseback riding delivers a feeling of freedom and a greater connection with nature.

3. Historical Sites: Ride to historical sites tucked in the proximity of river towns. Discover old castles, rural villages, and monuments that convey stories of the region's rich past.

4. Panoramic Views: Ascend to lofty spots for stunning panoramic views of the Danube. Enjoy the calm as you stare over the river's leisurely flow and the surrounding scenery.

5. Local Culture: Engage with the local equestrian community, experiencing the cultural importance of

horseback riding in the area. Some places may provide guided rides with informed residents.

6. Vineyard Excursions: In wine-producing areas, saddle up for rides through vineyards, where rows of grapevines offer a picturesque background. Some trips also include stops at local vineyards for samples.

7. Sunset Rides: Opt for sunset rides along the riverbanks, where the shifting hues of the sky give a magnificent light over the Danube. It's a calm and romantic way to finish a day of exploring.

Practical Tips:

- Ensure that you select a reputable horseback riding outfitter with well-trained horses and skilled guides.
- Wear proper apparel, including comfortable clothing and closed-toe shoes suited for riding.
- Check the difficulty level of the path to fit your riding expertise.
- Follow safety rules supplied by the outfitter to guarantee a secure and pleasurable trip.

Horseback riding near river cities along the Danube is not simply a leisure activity; it's a voyage that enables you to harmonize with nature, absorb local culture, and create lasting memories against the background of this renowned European waterway.

Savoring the Danube: Regional Cuisine Highlights

A Danube River cruise is more than simply a tour through history and scenery; it's also a gastronomic adventure that encourages you to sample the varied delicacies of the areas that line the riverbanks. Every curve of the Danube exposes you to new culinary traditions, delighting your taste senses with a symphony of regional delicacies.

1. Gastronomic Delights in Germany:
   - Start your German gastronomic trip with hearty sausages, pretzels, and sauerkraut.
   - Indulge in Bavarian delicacies like Schweinshaxe (roasted pork knuckle) and Weisswurst (white sausage).
   - Dive into the beer culture with a selection of local beers ranging from crisp lagers to powerful bocks.

2. Culinary Elegance in Austria:
   - Try the famed Wiener Schnitzel, a breaded and fried veal or pig cutlet from Austria.
   - Satisfy your sweet tooth with Sachertorte, a delicious chocolate cake, and Apfelstrudel, a traditional apple pastry.

- Complement your meals with famous Austrian wines that highlight the region's vineyard excellence.

3. Extravaganza of Hungarian Spices:
   - Savor the robust tastes of Hungarian cuisine with meals such as Goulash, a thick and flavorful stew.
   - Try classic Lángos, deep-fried flatbreads with sour cream and cheese on top.
   - Visit spice shops and sample paprika-infused dishes, which are popular in Hungarian cuisine.

4. Slovakian Culinary Treasures:
   - Try Haluky, Slovakia's version of gnocchi, which is often served with sheep cheese and bacon.
   - Indulge in substantial bean and sausage soups inspired by the country's rural culinary traditions.
   - Try local dairy products, such as bryndza cheese, which is used in many Slovakian cuisines.

5. Serbian Savory Dishes:
   - Dive into Serbian cuisine with evapi, which are grilled minced beef kebabs often eaten with flatbread.
   - Savor the distinct tastes of Ajvar, a peppery spice, and Kajmak, a creamy dairy spread.
   - Quench your thirst with Rakija, a fruit brandy popular across the Balkans.

6. Culinary Surprises in Romania:
- Try Mămăligă, a typical Romanian polenta that is often served with sour cream and cheese.
- Try Mici, grilled sausages seasoned with garlic and spices that are a popular street snack.
- Finish with Papanasi, a delectable dessert of fried doughnuts with sour cream and jam.

7. Culinary Traditions in Bulgaria:
- Banitsa, a Bulgarian pastry stuffed with cheese and eggs that represents the country's baking prowess, is a must-try.
- Try Kavarma, a slow-cooked stew with various meats and veggies.
- Try the Shopska Salad, a delicious combination of tomatoes, cucumbers, peppers, and feta.

Allow your taste senses to lead you as you cruise down the Danube, enabling the river's gastronomic symphony to dazzle you with a delicious selection of regional delicacies and genuine tastes.

Popular Regional Dishes

Austrian Wiener Schnitzel: A Culinary Classic

Wiener Schnitzel is an Austrian culinary staple whose simple but excellent preparation crosses boundaries. This meal, which is traditionally cooked with veal, contains a tenderized and breaded cutlet that is pan-fried to golden perfection. As a consequence, the crispy, golden skin envelops the juicy, delicious meat within.

Elements to Consider:
- Veal Cutlet: The original Wiener Schnitzel is produced from veal that has been pounded to a thin and consistent thickness. Variations using pork or chicken are also popular.
- Breading Method: The cutlet is first covered in flour, then in beaten eggs, and lastly in breadcrumbs. The dish's characteristic texture is enhanced by the thorough breading technique.
- Pan-Frying: The cutlet is pan-fried in clarified butter or oil until a lovely golden brown hue is achieved. This way of grilling offers a crispy surface while keeping the meat soft.
- Serving Style: Wiener Schnitzel is often served with a slice of lemon and a side of potato salad or parsley potatoes. The lemon's tangy bite gives a pleasant counterpoint to the dish's richness.

Wiener Schnitzel has a particular position in Austrian cuisine because it embodies the right blend of simplicity and refinement. It's more than simply a meal; it's a cultural experience that has left its stamp on dining tables throughout the globe, allowing everyone to appreciate Austria's culinary legacy.

Austrian Sachertorte: A Chocolate Delight

Sachertorte is a traditional Austrian dish known for its rich and decadent chocolate taste. This renowned Vienna cake is made up of layers of rich chocolate cake divided by a thin layer of apricot jam. Each slice is encased in a glossy, dark chocolate glaze, which adds a touch of luxury. Sachertorte has become a hallmark of Austrian patisserie skill and a must-try for tourists experiencing the country's culinary wonders, sometimes served with a dollop of unsweetened whipped cream.

Hungarian Goulash: A Hearty Hungarian Classic

Goulash, a traditional Hungarian cuisine, is a thick and savory stew with worldwide recognition. Goulash is a culinary masterpiece composed of soft pieces of meat, generally beef, slow-cooked with onions, paprika, and a mix of spices.

This robust recipe often includes potatoes, carrots, and bell peppers, resulting in a flavorful and comforting supper. Goulash, traditionally cooked over an open flame in a cauldron, encapsulates the spirit of Hungarian culinary traditions, delivering a sensation of comfort and powerful tastes.

Goulash, whether eaten in the busy markets of Budapest or quiet rural pubs, demonstrates Hungary's commitment to culinary quality and the art of slow cooking. Goulash is a hallmark of Hungarian hospitality and a must-try for anyone discovering the cuisines of the Danube area, thanks to its rich scent and unique taste.

Lángos: A Hungarian Deep-Fried Delight

Lángos is a famous Hungarian street snack with a crispy outside and a soft, doughy inside. This delicious delight starts with a basic dough of wheat, water, yeast, and salt. After rising, the dough is stretched into a thin, flat form and deep-fried till golden brown.

Lángos, which is traditionally served hot and fresh, may be eaten in a variety of ways. It's usually covered with a heavy layer of sour cream and shredded cheese, which gives it a rich and creamy texture. Toppings such as garlic, garlic butter, or a sprinkling of salt may be added for an extra taste.

Lángos is a flexible meal, and although the traditional form is still popular, new varieties with toppings like ham, bacon, or even Nutella have gained appeal. Lángos captures the delightful simplicity of Hungarian cuisine, whether consumed as a snack at a local market or as a filling street food alternative.

Haluky (Slovakia): A Delicious Culinary Tradition

Haluky, a popular Slovakian dish, is a substantial and comfortable dinner that highlights the country's rich culinary tradition. The uneven, gnocchi-like forms of these dumplings, cooked from grated potatoes and flour, set them apart. Haluky are noted for their exquisite chewiness and rustic texture after being boiled and then pan-fried.

Bryndzové Haluky is one of the most popular versions, in which the dumplings are lavishly covered with bryndza, a sour sheep cheese particular to the area. The meal is sometimes served with smoked bacon or sausage, which adds delicious depth to the taste profile.

Haluky has a particular position in Slovakian families, and it is commonly consumed during family gatherings, holidays, and cultural events. Its straightforward but gratifying character captures the spirit of traditional Slovakian comfort cuisine, providing a delectable and genuine flavor of the country's culinary traditions.

cevapi (Serbia): A Balkan Delight

The renowned Serbian meal evapi is a culinary jewel that embodies the rich tastes of the Balkan area. These little, grilled minced beef sausages are a Serbian culinary specialty, recognized for their savory flavor and unique technique. Evapi are molded into finger-sized cylinders before grilling and are often produced from a variety of ground meats—often a blend of beef and pork—seasoned with garlic, onions, and different spices. This meal is a lovely blend of smokey, grilled goodness and rich, savory accompaniments, served with somun (a kind of flatbread), chopped onions, and a dollop of kajmak (a creamy dairy spread). Evapi is a culinary experience that encapsulates the spirit of Serbian hospitality and gourmet history, whether consumed as street food or as part of a full dinner.

Mămăligă (Romania): Cornmeal Treat

Mămăligă is a classic Romanian dish with an important position in the country's culinary history. Mămăligă, also known as Romanian polenta, is produced with coarse yellow cornmeal, water, and salt. The mixture is heated until it becomes thick and porridge-like.

This adaptable meal may be served in a variety of ways:

1. Mămăligă is often served as a side dish to accompany stews, grilled meats, or sausages. Its mild taste contrasts well with more powerful main dishes.

2. Mămăligă might sometimes take center stage as a main dish. Layer it with cheese, sour cream, or butter for a delightful and warm supper.

3. Sweet Variations: Mămăligă may be sweetened with sugar and stacked with fruits, jams, or honey for a sweet dessert. This sweet variation is eaten as a dessert or for breakfast.

4. Grilled Mămăligă: Grilling slices of Mămăligă adds a wonderful smokiness and a crispy exterior, giving this classic meal a distinctive touch.

Mămăligă is a cultural emblem as well as a gastronomic treat, embodying the simplicity and inventiveness of Romanian cuisine. Its simple ingredients belie the rich and soothing experience it provides, making it a favorite on Romanian tables and a must-try for tourists discovering the region's unique tastes.

Bulgarian Banitsa: A Flaky Pastry Tradition

Banitsa is a traditional Bulgarian pastry that has become a hallmark of the country's culinary history. This classic treat is created by stacking thin filo pastry sheets with a mixture of whisked eggs, Bulgarian feta cheese (sirene), and sometimes yogurt. The layers are then cooked till brown, yielding a savory and delicious pastry.

Banitsa may be served in a variety of ways to suit different tastes and situations. To improve the taste profile, spinach, leeks, or minced beef are occasionally added. The meal is often served at special events, family gatherings, or as a favorite breakfast item when coupled with a dollop of yogurt.

Banitsa's exquisite flavor, along with its cultural importance, has made it a Bulgarian table staple. The meal exemplifies the country's dedication to maintaining culinary traditions while providing a delectable glimpse into Bulgarian hospitality and food.

Schweinshaxe (Germany): A Pork Lovers' Paradise

Schweinshaxe is a traditional German meal, especially popular in Bavaria. This delectable delicacy showcases the expertise of German pork cooking with a roasted ham hock. The crispy, crackling skin on the surface and soft, delicious meat on the interior distinguish this meal.

The ham hock is generally marinated or rubbed with a blend of spices, including garlic, caraway, and occasionally beer, to enhance the richness of the pork in Schweinshaxe. The hock is slow-cooked until the flesh is tender and the skin has a wonderful crispiness.

Schweinshaxe is generally served as a robust main dish with traditional sides like sauerkraut and potato dumplings. The mix of crispy skin, delicious meat, and fragrant spices makes this meal popular among people looking for a genuine taste of German cuisine, particularly in Bavaria's snug beer gardens and traditional pubs.

Weisswurst is a Bavarian delicacy.

Weisswurst, or "white sausage," is a typical Bavarian delicacy and a culinary emblem of Germany. This mild, white sausage is created with minced veal and back bacon and is seasoned with fresh parsley, mace, onions, ginger, and cardamom. The sausages, which are encased in a thin membrane, are boiled rather than grilled or fried, retaining their delicate taste and assuring a smooth texture.

Weisswurst is a meticulously prepared sausage that is generally served as a mid-morning meal, making it a staple of Bavarian breakfast or brunch. They're usually served with sweet mustard, pretzels, and a refreshing Weissbier (white beer).

Weisswurst has cultural importance in Bavaria, and eating it is a custom - the sausages are traditionally devoured before midday. This culinary jewel not only exemplifies Bavaria's dedication to its gastronomic legacy, but it also offers a great culinary experience for tourists discovering German food along the Danube's banks.

Serbian Rakija: A Spirited Tradition

Rakija, a traditional Serbian liquor, is a powerful fruit brandy with deep roots in the country's culinary and cultural traditions. This strong drink is historically created from different fruits, including plums (ljivovica), apricots, grapes, and others, by a distillation process.

Rakija, which has an alcohol concentration ranging from 40% to 60%, is often consumed at special events, family gatherings, and festivities. Its creation is a social event, with families and communities joining together to prepare and share this treasured elixir.

Each area in Serbia is proud of its own Rakija recipes, resulting in a wide range of tastes. Rakija, whether drank as an aperitif or used to toast, embodies the warmth and conviviality of Serbian hospitality. It is more than simply a drink; it represents brotherhood, tradition, and the essence of Serbian culture.

Papanasi (Romania): A Yummy Romanian Dessert

Papanasi are typical Romanian doughnuts that have a distinct position in the cuisine of the nation. These delectable sweets are created with cottage cheese, flour, eggs, and a splash of vanilla. The dough is formed into little, round dumplings with a central depression to hold different toppings.

Papanas are normally served warm and topped with a hefty dollop of sour cream and fruit jam, which is sometimes produced from berries such as sour cherries or raspberries. The contrast between the warm, somewhat crispy surface and the creamy core, as well as the explosion of fruity sweetness, makes Papanasi a popular dessert in Romania, where it is savored at a variety of events and festivals. Papanasi epitomizes the rich and wonderful tastes of Romanian cuisine, whether enjoyed as a warm delicacy or a spectacular dessert.

Kavarma (Bulgaria): A Harmonious Culinary Journey

Kavarma, a popular dish in Bulgarian cuisine, is a slow-cooked stew that reflects the region's rich tastes and traditions. Kavarma is a savory and flavorful meal that is often cooked with a range of meats such as hog, chicken, or lamb.

The meats are marinated in a variety of spices, which often include garlic, paprika, and herbs, infusing the meal with layers of flavorful depth. Tomatoes, peppers, and onions provide both freshness and sweetness to the stew, producing a harmonic balance of flavors.

The manner of preparation distinguishes Kavarma. Slow-cooking the marinated meats and veggies allows the flavors to mingle and enhance. This mild cooking method yields soft, succulent meats surrounded by a powerful and fragrant sauce.

Kavarma is often served boiling with a side of rice or crusty bread to mop up the luscious juices. The meal not only fills the stomach but also provides a sense of Bulgaria's culinary history, where the leisurely technique of cooking turns modest materials into a symphony of tastes that appeal to both residents and tourists.

Mici (Romania): Perfectly Grilled

Mici, commonly known as "mititei," is a popular Romanian meal that is adored by both residents and tourists alike. These little, grilled sausages are a gastronomic pleasure that's full of taste and heritage.

Mici, which are often produced from a mixture of minced meats—often a combination of pig, beef, and lamb—showcase Romania's proficiency in producing luscious, well-seasoned grilled meats.

Mici's particular flavor is achieved by a precise blend of garlic, black pepper, and different spices. The sausages are formed into compact cylindrical shapes before being cooked to perfection. As a consequence, the dish has a crispy surface and a juicy, savory inside.

Mici are often consumed in a casual, communal context, making them a great option for parties, festivals, and family picnics. Mici embodies the essence of Romanian gastronomy—a lovely blend of simplicity, intense tastes, and communal dining—served with mustard, fresh bread, and occasionally a side of pickles or fries.

Cruise Dining Recommendations

A Danube River cruise is more than simply a gorgeous journey; it's also a gastronomic experience set against the background of Europe's cultural riches. Here are some eating suggestions to help you enjoy every minute of your cruise:

1. Gastronomic Delights on Board:
- Indulge in the cruise ship's various restaurants, which include a mix of foreign and regional food.

- Attend thematic dining events that highlight the gastronomic delights of the Danube's many civilizations.

2. Tastings of Local Cuisine:
- Take advantage of onboard samples to get acquainted with the cuisine of each destination. As part of immersive experiences, sample local wines, cheeses, and delicacies.

3. Dining al fresco on the deck:
- Dine on the outside deck while enjoying panoramic views as you travel past attractive towns and gorgeous landscapes.

4. Specialty Dining Experiences:
- Attend unique dining events like a sunset supper or a BBQ night on the terrace. These encounters offer a magical touch to your gastronomic excursion.

5. Exploring Local Restaurants:
- During port pauses, explore the towns along the Danube to sample real local food. Your cruise line may provide guided culinary tours or restaurant suggestions.

6. Workshops and demonstrations in the kitchen:
- Participate in culinary courses or demonstrations given by local chefs aboard. Learn how to make traditional delicacies and take home a taste of your Danube adventure.

7. Dietary Preferences Customized:

- Inform the cruise personnel in advance of any food preferences or limitations. Most cruise lines are accommodative and may modify meals to special requirements.

8. Options for Casual and Fine Dining:
- Enjoy the best of both worlds by mixing casual and exquisite eating. Casual dining alternatives give a comfortable environment for more formal gatherings, whilst fine dining nights provide an exquisite setting for more formal affairs.

9. Celebratory Dining Experiences:
- Celebrate important events with bespoke dining experiences aboard. The cruise team may create unforgettable dining experiences for you, whether it's a birthday, anniversary, or just a milestone in your voyage.

10. Taking Advantage of Local Markets:
- If your cruise itinerary includes stops at local markets, peruse the bright booths selling fresh vegetables, handcrafted goods, and regional delights. It's an opportunity to interact with the culinary culture on a more personal level.

Remember that eating on a Danube cruise is more than simply food; it's an essential element of the whole experience.

Let your taste buds become fellow passengers on this gastronomic adventure down the Danube, whether you're relishing a gourmet dinner on deck, discovering onshore eateries, or participating in culinary activities.

Famous Cities and Towns

Vienna, Austria: A Cultural and Elegance Symphony

Stepping to the Danube in Vienna was like entering a great artwork. The city, which was a seamless combination of royal beauty and artistic attraction, left an everlasting imprint on my Danube River voyage.

I was fascinated by the beautiful blend of history and contemporary as I wandered along the cobblestone alleys. Vienna presented itself as a city in constant communication with its history and future, from the opulent grandeur of the Hofburg Palace to the modern pulse of the MuseumsQuartier.

Highlights:

1. Schloss Schönbrunn:
- Schönbrunn Palace's splendor took me to the Habsburg period. The opulent apartments and pristine grounds reverberated with stories of imperial grandeur, providing a look into royalty's life.

2. The Cathedral of St. Stephen:
- The Gothic spires of St. Stephen's Cathedral reached toward the skies. Inside, I was amazed by the exquisite

stained glass windows and the panoramic view from the South Tower.

3. The Belvedere Palace
- Belvedere Palace, a work of beauty in Baroque architecture, hosted a magnificent collection of Austrian art. The famed Klimt paintings, notably "The Kiss," gave another level of creative brilliance to my visit to Vienna.

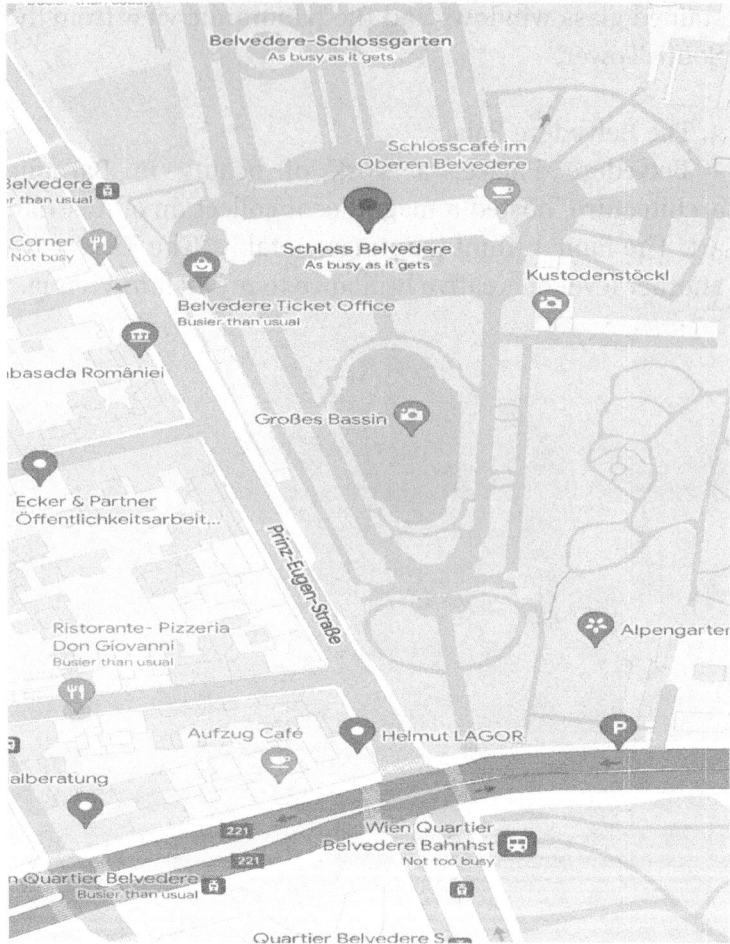

4. Coffee Shop Culture:
- I spent lazy days in ancient cafés, embracing Vienna's legendary coffeehouse culture. Sipping a melange and eating a piece of Sachertorte were routines that allowed me to absorb the spirit of the city.

5. State Opera of Vienna:
- An evening at the Vienna State Opera was the highlight of my trip. The venue's ageless beauty, combined with a performance that echoed the city's musical tradition, offered an extraordinary cultural immersion.

6. Naschmarkt:
- Naschmarkt, a bustling market in Vienna that entices with a kaleidoscope of tastes. Exploring the market becomes a sensory trip through gastronomic pleasures, from fresh vegetables to overseas specialties.

7. MuseumsQuartier:
- MuseumsQuartier, a cultural center set in medieval courtyards, lured with contemporary art galleries and chic shops. The contrast between modern ingenuity against historic buildings exemplified Vienna's dynamic vitality.

Every cobblestone in Vienna appeared to reverberate with Mozartian echoes and the beauty of the waltz. It wasn't simply a city to me; it was a symphony of elegance and culture, tempting me to waltz along its historic streets and appreciate the ageless beauty of the Danube's banks.

Linz, Austria: A Cultural Riverside Symphony

As my Danube River cruise arrived in Linz, Austria, I discovered a city that perfectly mixes ancient elegance with contemporary life. The riverfront setting and the city's cultural gems made for an amazing chapter in my travels.

Linz greeted me with lovely old-world buildings that lined the riverbanks. I encountered picturesque squares and attractive cafés where inhabitants exchanged enthusiastic discussions over coffee and pastries while wandering around the cobblestone streets of Old Town.

The Ars Electronica Center, a futuristic center of interactive displays investigating the interaction of art, technology, and society, was a highlight of my Linz visit. The startling modernism of this core provided a strong but harmonic contrast to the city's historic towers.

Highlights of the city include:
1. Charms of Linz's Old Town: Strolling around Linz's Old Town (Altstadt) was like entering into a fairy tale. The vivid façade of Gothic and Baroque buildings offered a stunning setting for exploring.

2. The Lentos Art Museum, which overlooks the Danube, has an exceptional collection of modern and contemporary art. The sleek glass façade mimicked the flow of the river, providing a dynamic contrast to the city's historic heart.

3. Brucknerhaus Concert Hall: The Brucknerhaus Concert Hall is located in Linz, a city with a rich musical history. Even if you don't see a performance, the

architecture and riverbank setting make it a cultural treasure to see.

4. Linz Taste: Tasting the native food was a great experience. Linzer Torte, a popular Austrian delicacy, was a sweet pleasure, and traditional Austrian coffee houses offered a nice location to savor it.

5. Pöstlingberg City Views: I climbed Pöstlingberg by the famed Linz Grotto Railway, which provides panoramic views of the city and the Danube. The lovely pilgrimage chapel atop the hill lent a historical touch to the picturesque scene.

Linz, with its mix of antiquity and modernity, quickly became a favorite stop on my Danube adventure. The city's dedication to preserving its cultural heritage while embracing modernity generated an environment that made me appreciate Austria's capacity to reconcile the past and the present.

Melk, Austria: A Danube Baroque Gem

As the cruise ship cruised into the gorgeous town of Melk, Austria, I found myself enveloped in a scenario straight out of a fantasy. Melk is a baroque marvel hidden along the Danube's banks, and my own experience here was nothing short of amazing.

Highlights:

1. Melk monastery (Stift Melk): Melk's crown treasure is unquestionably its magnificent monastery built on a hill above the town. The abbey's golden colors and magnificent baroque architecture spread before me as I climbed the main staircase. The library, with its antique manuscripts and murals, transported me to a time of intellectual affluence.

2. Melk's riverfront atmosphere is a postcard-worthy setting. The shoreline is lined with charming cottages with flower-filled balconies, providing a peaceful setting for a leisurely promenade. Cafés near the river are ideal for savoring a coffee while viewing the Danube's calm currents.

3. Views of the Wachau Valley: Melk serves as an entrance to the Wachau Valley, a UNESCO World Heritage site known for its wineries and sceneries. Melk's panoramic vistas of undulating hills and terraced vineyards are breathtakingly magnificent, offering a peek into Austria's lush beauty.

4. Local Flavors: Exploring Melk isn't complete until you try the local delights. I was able to indulge in apricot delicacies, a regional specialty. The town's gastronomic offerings echoed the sweetness of its surroundings, from apricot preserves to pastries.

5. Markets & Town Square: The town square is charming with its pastel-colored buildings and bustling ambiance. On market days, you'll discover booths bursting with

fresh vegetables, handcrafted goods, and a colorful display of local life.

My favorite memory from Melk was standing in the abbey's courtyard, surrounded by centuries-old walls that rang with history's whispers. The contrast of the abbey's grandeur against the tranquil Danube countryside made an unforgettable impression on my tour. Melk emanated a timeless fascination that made it a genuine highlight of my Danube River trip, whether meandering around the town's cobblestone alleys or staring at the river from the abbey's terrace.

Dürnstein, Austria: A Danube Treasure

Dürnstein, located in the Wachau Valley, is a lovely Austrian town that captivates visitors with its medieval splendor and gorgeous views. Dürnstein appeared as a beautiful jewel during my Danube River trip, leaving an unforgettable imprint on my vacation.

Dürnstein revealed itself like a fairytale hamlet when the cruise liner parked gently down the Danube. Cobblestone lanes led me across town to the renowned blue and white church tower that dominates the skyline. The air was filled with the delicious aroma of blossoming vines from adjacent vineyards, making it an appealing sight.

I took a trip through the small lanes, uncovering centuries-old cottages decked with vivid flowers. The town emanated a tranquil vibe that beckoned me to discover its history and take in the scenery.

Highlights:

1. Dürnstein Abbey: The Augustinian Abbey, a majestic monument with a history extending back to the 15th century, is the town's focal point. The architecture of the monastery and the quiet courtyard create a peaceful atmosphere.

2. The remains of Kuenringer Castle, perched on a hill above Dürnstein, provide panoramic views of the Danube Valley. The ascent to the castle is rewarded with stunning views, making it a must-see.

3. Dürnstein is bordered by vineyards and apricot orchards, which contribute to the region's renown for wine and apricot products. Tasting local wines and indulging in apricot treats became a highlight of my trip.

4. Dürnstein is located in the Wachau Valley, a UNESCO World Heritage Site recognized for its breathtaking vistas. The vineyard-covered slopes, flowing rivers, and old villages combine to provide an enthralling landscape.

5. Artisan stores & Cafés: The streets of the town are lined with artisan stores that sell local goods and souvenirs. Cafés with outside seating are ideal for

enjoying Austrian coffee and pastries while taking in the atmosphere of the town.

Dürnstein seemed like a time capsule, with its timeless charm and rich cultural legacy. It was a highlight of my Danube River trip since it provided a great combination of history, natural beauty, and friendly friendliness. As the sun fell behind the hills, throwing a warm light over the village, I felt I had uncovered a hidden gem along the Danube's meandering route.

Budapest, Hungary: An Elegance and History Tapestry

Budapest appeared on the horizon as the Danube gently caressed our cruise ship, a city that easily mixes the grandeur of its history with the frenetic pulse of contemporary life. When I stepped into the cobblestone streets, I was engulfed in a vibrant symphony of culture, architecture, and genuine welcome.

Our voyage started with a walk over Budapest's famed Chain Bridge, a tribute to the city's architectural brilliance. The city's lights lighted the Danube as the sun set, providing a magnificent glow over the river. The view from the bridge surrounded Buda Castle, towering atop Castle Hill—a stunning spectacular that set the tone for our Budapest excursion.

Ascending Castle Hill, we visited Fisherman's Bastion's fanciful spires and terraces. The sweeping views of the city below were spectacular, providing an ideal background for photographs of Budapest's architectural gems. Matthias Church, nearby, stood as a timeless beauty, its brilliant tiles and Gothic spires narrating tales from years past.

A trip to Budapest would be completed without a visit to the city's famous thermal spas. Gellért Baths, located on the Buda side, proved to be a relaxing getaway. I marveled at the Art Nouveau buildings around me as I buried myself in the warm waves. Gellért Hill, capped with the Liberty Statue, offered a postcard-worthy perspective of the city, encapsulating Budapest's mix of history and contemporary vibrancy.

We examined the grandeur of Budapest's avenue, Andrássy Avenue, which is a UNESCO World Heritage site. The Hungarian State Opera House and the beautiful homes along the road were testaments to the city's wealthy history. The voyage ended in the Hungarian Parliament, a gleaming architectural beauty reflecting the city's political significance and adherence to democratic values.

We went down the Danube Promenade as night fell, enjoying the city's sights bathed in a mellow light. The Parliament building, Buda Castle, and the bridges took on a new personality, emanating an enchantment. We chose a Danube night cruise and floated under the dazzling lights, leaving memories of Budapest's splendor imprinted on the canvas of the night sky.

Budapest made an unforgettable imprint on my Danube tour with its seamless combination of history, culture, and current vitality. It was a city that called to my soul—a location where every turn revealed a new chapter in Hungary's rich history, asking me to be a part of it.

Nuremberg, Germany: A Historical and Charming Tapestry

My visit to Nuremberg on my Danube River trip made an unforgettable imprint, tying together the strands of history, culture, and modern appeal. The city captured me from the minute I walked into its cobblestone streets, with its medieval beauty and strong soul.

Nuremberg is a living witness to Germany's rich history. The Imperial Castle, set on a hill, offers tourists the chance to explore its well-preserved rooms and wander over centuries-old walls. The renowned Nuremberg Castle and the towering Gothic façade of St. Lorenz Church took me back in time as I went around the Old Town.

Nuremberg has a profound role in contemporary history as the location of the Nuremberg Trials after World War II. The Palace of Justice, where the trials were held, emanates solemnity. I had a tremendous feeling of contemplation on the quest of justice while being in the courtroom where history transpired.

The Market Square, or Hauptmarkt, in Nuremberg, is a lively center where the city's heart pulses most vigorously. The area is framed by the Frauenkirche, with its magnificent façade, and the famed Schöner Brunnen, a wonderfully ornamented fountain. The market was filled with kiosks selling everything from local crafts to scented spices during my visit, providing a sensory feast.

Nuremberg is famous for gastronomic pleasures, and I couldn't pass up the local delicacy, Nuremberg sausages. These tasty sausages became a culinary highlight, relished in the lovely environment of traditional beer gardens when served with sauerkraut and mustard.

Nuremberg displayed a new revival beyond its ancient sites. The Documentation Center Nazi Party Rally Grounds offered a harsh but necessary look into the city's participation during the Nazi period. This museum's contemporary design reflects the city's dedication to confronting its complicated past.

In essence, Nuremberg is a city that seamlessly merges the ancient with the modern, providing a mosaic of experiences for every visitor. Nuremberg is a multidimensional treasure along the Danube, beckoning investigation, introspection, and a true appreciation for its indomitable character, from the echoes of the past behind its castle walls to the bustling vitality of its marketplaces.

Regensburg, Germany: A Historical River Tapestry

Regensburg, nestled on the Danube's banks, appeared before me like a fairytale village, each cobblestone street whispering stories of a bygone past. The city opened with a compelling combination of history and charm as I strolled through its well-preserved medieval core.

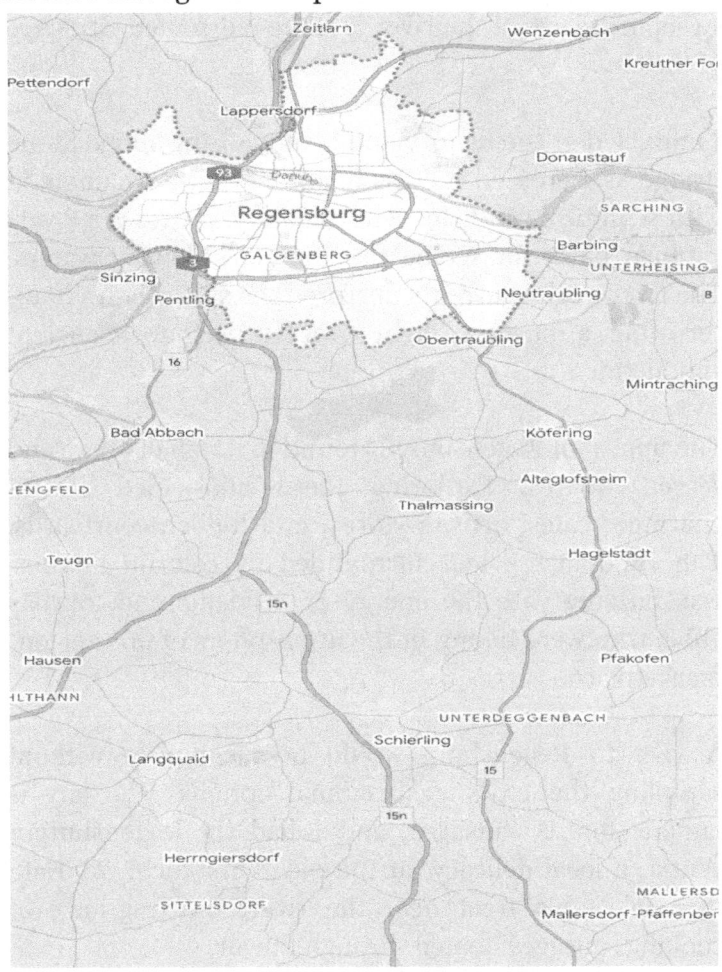

Regensburg's heart is a UNESCO World Heritage site, and it's simple to understand why. With its pointed spires and half-timbered dwellings, medieval architecture provides a timeless mood. St. Peter's Cathedral, a Gothic masterpiece, stands as a tribute to the city's religious past. Climbing the towers provided sweeping views of the river and the red-roofed cityscape of the city.

I marveled at the history and beauty of the famed Stone Bridge as I crossed it. This historic bridge, ornamented with sculptures and steeped in history, provides a lovely vantage point for seeing the Danube's flowing waters. The river's calm currents mirrored the sunset sun's hues, throwing a pleasant light over Regensburg's ancient silhouette.

The appeal of Regensburg is found in its small alleys and secret squares. Exploring these nooks led me to charming cafés, artisan stores, and hidden courtyards. The Haidplatz place, surrounded by colorful facades, was buzzing with the energy of residents and tourists alike, who were taking in the atmosphere of this ancient marketplace.

A visit to Regensburg would be incomplete without sampling the city's gastronomic options. The city is famous for its sausages, and I had the Regensburger Wurst, a local delicacy, at the old Wurstkuchl. As I ate this delectable treat near the river, the fragrance of cooking sausages floated through the air.

Regensburg mixes its ancient past with a thriving cultural scene. Among the medieval constructions are museums, galleries, and theaters. Thurn und Taxis Palace, a historic royal home, displayed the city's aristocratic heritage and provided a look into bygone ages' luxury.

Regensburg is, in essence, a living painting where the past and present collide. Its beauty is found not only in architectural marvels but also in the daily rhythms of life that unfold along the Danube. As I say goodbye to this lovely city, I carried not just recollections of its sights, but also a feeling of having entered a live chapter of European history.

Passau, Germany: A Riverfront Treasure

Passau, located at the confluence of the Danube, Inn, and Ilz rivers, is a mesmerizing city that combines history, culture, and scenic scenery. Passau created an unforgettable effect on me, combining picturesque cobblestone lanes, architectural splendors, and the relaxing rhythm of running streams.

Walking through the Old Town of Passau seemed like going back in time. The St. Stephen's Cathedral was a visual wonder, with its unique baroque design and the world's biggest cathedral organ. Each corner offered a narrative engraved in the city's rich history as I explored the meandering streets, old mansions, and lovely squares.

The confluence of the three rivers imparted a particular tranquility to Passau. Riverside promenades were ideal for a leisurely walk, enabling me to take in the tranquil vistas of the flowing streams and the exquisite bridges that spanned the riverbanks. It was a place to take a break, think, and take in the natural beauty that surrounded the city.

Passau's dedication to the arts was obvious in its thriving cultural scene. The Glass Museum, which displayed elaborate glasswork, and the modern galleries lent a modern touch to the city's traditional environment. I was able to attend a classical performance in the magnificent rooms of the Bishop's Residence, which increased my admiration for Passau's cultural wealth.

A boat journey down the Inn River provides a new perspective on Passau's splendor. With each bend, the riverbank panorama emerged, while the lecture gave insights into the city's past. The crystal-clear waters of the Inn River matched the metropolis, providing a tranquil and invigorating experience.

The food scene in Passau is enticed with tiny cafés and eateries nestled away in picturesque nooks. I savored regional delicacies, drinking coffee by the river and tasting Bavarian specialties. It was a gastronomic excursion that reflected the city's warm welcome and dedication to cultural preservation.

Passau, in essence, enthralled me—a city where history whispers through cobblestone alleyways, the Danube's embrace adds a rhythmic tune, and cultural fusion weaves a vibrant tapestry. Passau is a jewel on the Danube, beckoning guests to immerse themselves in its timeless appeal, whether exploring its architectural treasures, eating local cuisine, or just soaking in riverbank peace.

Bratislava, Slovakia: Danube's Whimsical Charm

Bratislava, nestled along the Danube's banks, greeted me with a mix of medieval elegance and dynamic vitality. The city displayed its personality as I explored the cobblestone streets and prominent sites, leaving a lasting impact on my Danube tour.

I was transported to a fairy-tale environment when walking around the Old Town. A charming mood was produced by the charming squares, pastel-colored houses, and small alleyways. The imposing presence of Bratislava Castle atop a hill enhanced the city's skyline.

St. Michael's Gate, the sole remaining medieval city gate, was one of the highlights. Climbing to the observation platform provided me with magnificent views of the Danube River and surrounding area. The contrast of antique structures and contemporary metropolis was a visual feast.

As twilight fell, I made my way to the SNP Bridge's UFO Observation Deck. The lights of the city reflected on the Danube, creating a lovely atmosphere. Bratislava's ability to perfectly integrate its rich past with contemporary, energetic energy struck me here.

Highlights of the city include:
1. Explore Bratislava Castle, a majestic stronghold with a history reaching back to the 9th century. The castle not only provides historical insights but also provides spectacular views of the city and the river.

2. Old Town Square: Stroll around the lovely squares, which are alive with colorful architecture, outdoor cafés, and street performers. The Main Square, in particular, is a bustling center of activity.

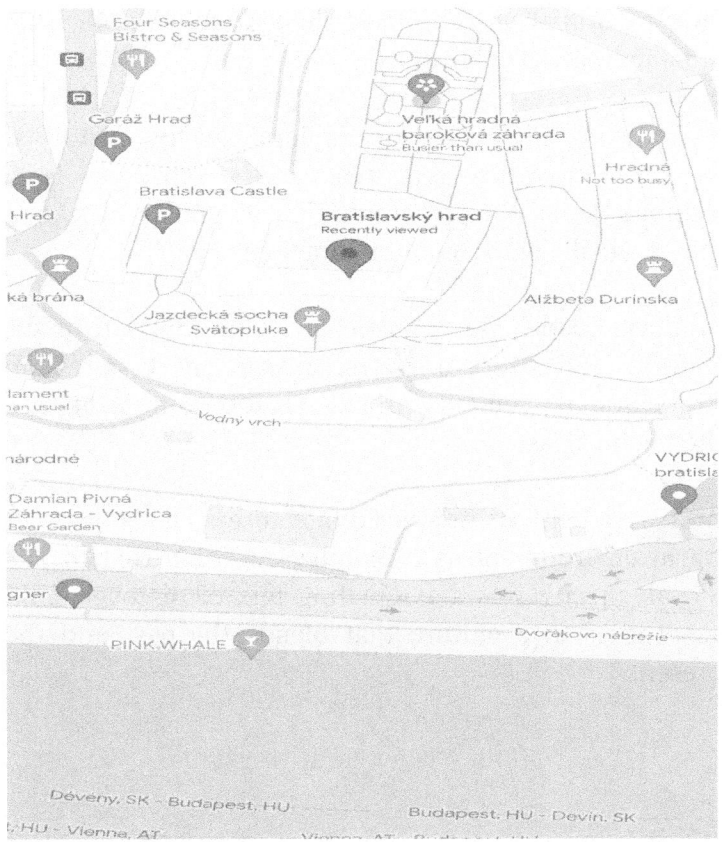

3. St. Martin's Cathedral: Admire the Gothic magnificence of Bratislava's St. Martin's Cathedral. Its tower dominates the skyline, and the inside is filled with fascinating historical items.

4. UFO Observation Deck: Take a once-in-a-lifetime excursion to the top of the SNP Bridge for a panoramic

view of Bratislava. The UFO-shaped building offers an outstanding view of the city.

5. Bratislava City Museum: Explore the city's history at the museum, which is situated in the Old Town Hall. Exhibits depict the transformation of Bratislava from a medieval village to a contemporary city.

6. Devn Castle: Devn Castle is at the junction of the Danube and Morava rivers, only a short sail from Bratislava. Its remains provide an intriguing peek into the region's past.

Bratislava, with its unique architecture, rich history, and warm environment, is a Danube jewel. My visit to this Slovakian city was a fascinating mix of discovery and absorption in a culture that blends the past and the present.

Off the Beaten Path Treasures

Czech Republic: esk Krumlov: Bohemian Fairytale

esk Krumlov, located in the gorgeous South Bohemian area of the Czech Republic, is a charming village that seems like a step into a medieval fairy tale. Its historical significance and well-preserved architecture make it a hidden treasure worth investigating.

Highlights include:

1. esk Krumlov Castle: This UNESCO World Heritage monument dominates the town's skyline and is a huge edifice with Gothic, Renaissance, and Baroque components. The castle provides breathtaking views of the Vltava River and the city below.

2. Old Town Plaza: The plaza is the beating center of Esk Krumlov, a labyrinth of small lanes flanked by magnificent Renaissance and Baroque structures. The

area's bustling ambiance is enhanced by charming stores, cafés, and artisan boutiques.

3. Views of the Vltava River: A stroll along the Vltava River, which runs through town, affords postcard-worthy scenery. The town's lovely atmosphere is enhanced by the historic Moldau River Bridge and attractive riverfront residences.

4. Eggenberg Brewery: Visit Eggenberg Brewery to learn about the local beer culture. Take a guided tour of the brewery to learn about the brewing process and sample traditional Czech beers in a historic setting.

5. Egon Schiele Art Centrum in Esk Krumlov: Art lovers may visit this center devoted to the works of Egon Schiele, an Austrian painter linked with the Expressionist style.

6. Rafting on the Vltava: Consider a leisurely rafting ride down the Vltava River for a fresh view of Esk Krumlov. This leisure activity enables you to experience the beauty of the town from a fresh perspective.

7. Krumlov Mill: Nestled near the castle, Krumlov Mill is a charming site where you may enjoy a tranquil riverbank setting and perhaps a meal or coffee.

8. esk Krumlov Puppet Museum: This eccentric museum showcases a collection of marionettes and

puppetry-related antiques, allowing visitors to discover the charm of traditional Czech puppetry.

esk Krumlov offers tourists to journey back in time with its cobblestone streets, ancient buildings, and a feeling of timelessness. Every aspect of this Bohemian town reveals a narrative of history, art, and magic, whether you're roaming around the castle grounds or drinking coffee in a riverbank café.

Szentendre, Hungary: A Danube Art Enclave

With its artistic attractiveness and vivid atmosphere, Szentendre, a lovely town perched along the Danube Bend, steals the hearts of tourists. Szentendre is a living painting, with small cobblestone alleyways leading to art galleries, attractive cafés, and centuries-old buildings.

Highlights:

1. Szentendre is known as a "museum town" because of its plethora of museums and galleries. Visit the Margit Kovács Ceramic Museum and the Ferenczy Museum, both of which showcase Hungarian art.

2. Baroque Churches: Take in some of the town's baroque buildings, such as the Blagovestenska Church and the Serbian Orthodox Church. Each structure conveys a tale about Szentendre's many cultural influences.

3. Skansen Open-Air Museum: Travel back in time at the Skansen Open-Air Museum, which preserves typical Hungarian village life. Historic structures, such as a windmill and a press house, provide an insight into rural tradition.

4. Main Square (F tér): Szentendre's center, surrounded by pastel-colored buildings, artisan stores, and welcoming cafés. It's a great place to take in the vibe of the town.

5. Danube Promenade: Take a stroll along the Danube Promenade for beautiful views of the river and neighboring countryside. The riverside provides a peaceful respite from the town's busy streets.

6. Marzipan Museum: Visit the Marzipan Museum to satisfy your sweet craving, where culinary art takes the shape of beautiful marzipan sculptures. It's a delightful experience for both art and dessert connoisseurs.

7. Kovács Margit Square is a refuge for artists and art enthusiasts. Browse through galleries displaying a wide range of artworks, from paintings to sculptures, and possibly discover a one-of-a-kind item to bring home.

Szentendre's unique combination of creative energy, cultural history, and riverbank attractiveness distinguishes it as a hidden jewel along the Danube, enticing visitors to explore its picturesque streets and immerse themselves in the creativity that characterizes this delightful Hungarian town.

Novi Sad, Serbia: Serbia's Danube Jewel

Novi Sad, located on the banks of the Danube, is a cultural jewel that combines history, energetic vitality, and artistic beauty. Novi Sad, Serbia's second-largest city, encourages visitors to discover its rich past and join in the dynamic environment that distinguishes this Danubian destination.

Highlights include:

1. Petrovaradin stronghold: This 18th-century stronghold dominates the skyline and gives panoramic views of the city and the Danube. The stronghold, which houses the distinctive clock tower, organizes cultural events like as the renowned EXIT music festival.

2. Old Town and Dunavska Street: Stroll through the Old Town's small lanes, where Baroque architecture meets bohemian flare. Dunavska Street, which is dotted with cafés and stores, is ideal for a leisurely walk.

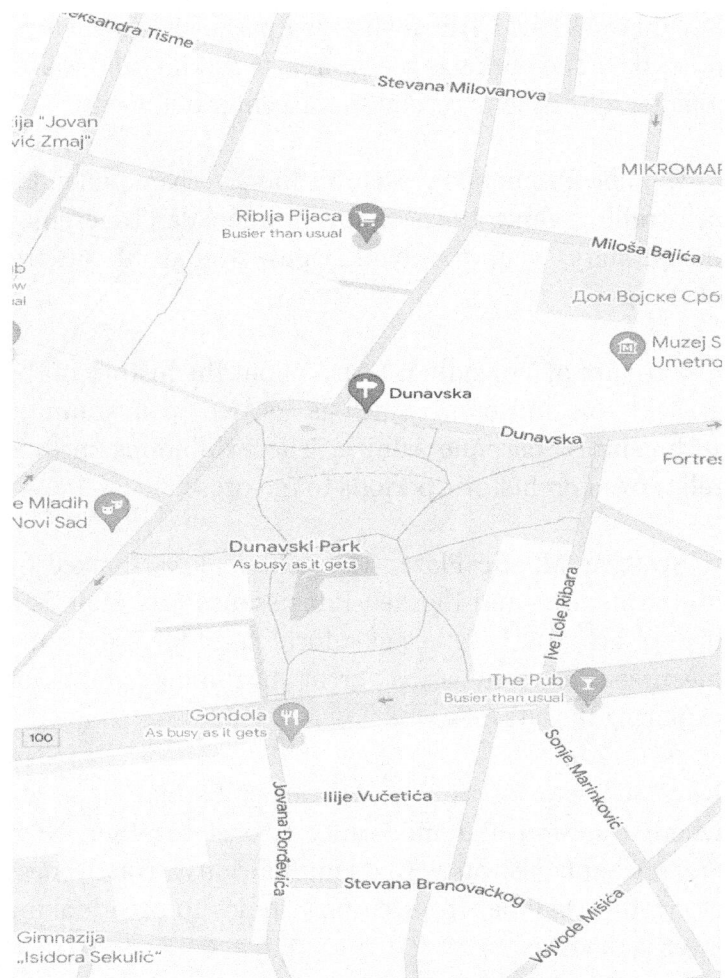

3. Admire the gorgeous architecture of this Orthodox cathedral, which is famed for its elaborate paintings and spectacular dome. The church bears witness to Novi Sad's religious and artistic history.

4. Dunavski Park: This lush green paradise is ideal for a quiet day. The park has sculptures, fountains, and walks, making it a peaceful retreat in the center of the city.

5. Danube Promenade: Take in the riverbank splendor by strolling along the Danube Promenade. Take enjoy the scenery, visit riverbank cafés, and drink up the bustling vibe.

6. Museum of Vojvodina: Learn about the history of the area at this museum, which is located in a stunning 18th-century baroque edifice. The exhibitions include relics from prehistoric periods to the present.

7. Svetozar Miletic Plaza: The center plaza, flanked by fine structures and the neo-Renaissance City Hall, is a hive of activity. It serves as a focal point for events and meetings, as well as a great beginning point for exploring the city.

Novi Sad, known as the "Athens of Serbia," is a city where tradition and modernity coexist together. Novi Sad enchants visitors with its multifarious attractiveness along the Danube, from cultural relics to breathtaking riverbank vistas.

Veliko Tarnovo, Bulgaria: Bulgarian History Citadel

Veliko Tarnovo, nestled on the Yantra River, rises like a medieval masterpiece, echoing stories of Bulgaria's rich past. This often-overlooked hidden treasure provides a compelling combination of architectural marvels, spectacular scenery, and a bustling cultural environment.

Highlights include:

1. Tsarevets Fortress: Veliko Tarnovo, crowned by the majestic Tsarevets Fortress, encourages tourists to travel back in time. The stronghold atop a hill not only offers panoramic views of the city but also holds ancient buildings including the Patriarchal Cathedral.

2. Samovodska Charshia: Stroll through the cobblestone lanes of Samovodska Charshia, an artisan's district that has retained its 19th-century beauty. Traditional workshops, stores, and restaurants display the artistry and friendliness of Bulgaria.

3. Admire the magnificent Asen's Monument, an emblem of the medieval Asen dynasty. It is situated on a hill and provides a different view of Veliko Tarnovo's attractive surroundings.

4. Sound & Light Show: At Tsarevets Fortress, the hypnotic Sound and Light Show brings the city's history to life with colorful illuminations, music, and narrative.

5. Gurko Street: Stroll along Gurko Street, which is lined with colorful residences and offers a nostalgic excursion into Veliko Tarnovo's architectural past.

6. Architectural Reserves: Visit architectural reserves such as Arbanasi, where well-preserved buildings and churches reflect the region's Renaissance splendor.

Veliko Tarnovo, with its hilltop strongholds, meandering lanes, and distinct sense of history, is a hidden gem awaiting discovery by anyone looking for a Bulgarian experience.

Iron Gates: The Majestic Danube Gorge

The Iron Gates is a spectacular natural marvel located along the Danube River, separating Serbia and Romania. This beautiful ravine formed through the Carpathian Mountains is a hidden treasure with spectacular vistas and historical importance.

Highlights include:

1. Geological Wonder: The Iron Gates Canyon is a tribute to nature's might, with towering limestone cliffs rising suddenly from the river. As the Danube flows through the small path, the sheer enormity of the canyon produces a spectacular scene.

2. Decebalus Statue: Marvel at the gigantic rock sculpture of Decebalus, Dacia's final ruler. This enormous sculpture carved into the rock provides a sense of ancient heritage to the environment.

3. Tabula Traiana: On the Serbian side of the canyon, see the Tabula Traiana, a Roman monument. This marble plaque celebrates the construction of a Roman route and offers insight into the region's historical ties.

4. A Danube River tour via the Iron Gates provides a front-row experience of this natural beauty. The tour travels through the narrowest and most breathtaking section of the canyon, enabling guests to take in the breathtaking scenery.

5. Natural Reserves: The Iron Gates area is rich in flora and animals. Nature lovers will enjoy the unspoiled wildness of Djerdap National Park in Serbia and the Iron Gates Natural Park in Romania.

6. Rural towns: Along the Danube's banks, you'll come across picturesque towns where time appears to stand still. These secret communities provide a look into traditional life in this isolated yet beautiful region of Europe.

The Iron Gates, with their beautiful combination of natural beauty and historical relics, allows visitors to go off the main road and see a less-explored aspect of the Danube's wonderful voyage.

Castle Heights and Riverside Tranquility in Visegrád, Hungary

Visegrád, located in the Danube Bend, is a captivating Hungarian jewel that combines history, natural beauty, and cultural appeal.

Highlights:

1. Visegrád Castle: Perched on a hill, the historic Visegrád Castle provides breathtaking views of the Danube River. Explore its medieval remains, which include the famous Solomon Tower.

2. The Royal Palace of Visegrád's ruins reflect the magnificence of Hungary's medieval nobility. Wander the medieval walls and envision the royal history that once existed there.

3. Danube Bend Views: Visegrád's picturesque splendor goes beyond its ancient landmarks. Below, the Danube Bend spreads, creating a stunning background for the town and its monuments.

4. Solomon's Tower: A hike to the castle complex's Solomon's Tower rewards you with unmatched views of the surrounding area. It's an ideal location for capturing the spirit of the Danube's meandering flow.

5. Visegrád Citadel: Explore the Visegrád Citadel by descending to the riverbed. This stronghold, hidden in a beautiful green location, provides a peaceful retreat with riverbank walks and calm vistas.

6. The Royal Residence Museum provides insight into Hungary's royal history via displays that describe the life of medieval kings and queens that once adorned Visegrád.

7. The Esztergom Basilica, Hungary's biggest church, is just a short distance away and beckons with its spectacular architectural and cultural importance.

Visegrád, with its historic fascination and natural beauty, is a hidden jewel along the Danube—a site where the river's timeless flow meets vestiges of Hungary's royal past.

Onboard Experience

Themed Gala Nights: Elegance and Entertainment Afloat

Themed Gala Nights on a Danube River cruise bring a touch of luxury and excitement to the onboard experience. These extraordinary nights are meant to immerse guests in a world of luxury, entertainment, and cultural enrichment.

Key Elements:

1. Dress Code: Themed Gala Nights sometimes come with a special dress code, encouraging passengers to wear beautiful apparel by the selected theme. Whether it's a black-tie dinner or a costume-themed gathering, travelers have the chance to express their flair.

2. Fine Dining: Gala Nights are complimented by spectacular dining experiences. The ship's culinary crew produces customized meals including gourmet treats, complementing the occasion with culinary perfection.

3. Entertainment: From live music performances to dance shows, Themed Gala Nights provide a broad selection of entertainment. Professional performers may

grace the stage, presenting passengers with an exquisite experience as they enjoy the night's celebrations.

4. Decor and Ambiance: The ship's interior is altered to reflect the theme of the evening. Lavish décor, ambient lighting, and meticulously chosen details create an immersive ambiance, transporting travelers to a realm of magic.

5. Cultural Immersion: Themed Gala Nights frequently feature aspects of the local culture or the cultural attractions of the cruise itinerary. This helps travelers to enhance their connection to the locations they are experiencing.

6. Photography Opportunities: Passengers may capture the enchantment of the evening with onboard photography services. The ship's photographers may provide professional picture sessions, giving guests lasting memories of the spectacular celebration.

Whether it's a traditional masquerade, a celebration of local customs, or a reference to the elegance of a bygone era, Themed Gala Nights on a Danube River cruise infuse the voyage with an additional layer of magic, creating unique experiences for all on board.

Onboard Entertainment Shows: A Riveting Cruise Experience

Onboard entertainment presentations on a Danube River cruise enrich your voyage with intriguing performances that merge culture, music, and narrative. These performances are created to enrich your nights and give a lovely ambiance while you travel down the historic river.

Key Features:

Variety entertainment: Enjoy a broad choice of entertainment, from live music and dance to dramatic shows. The onboard entertainment appeals to a variety of preferences, ensuring there's something for everyone.

Cultural Showcases: Immerse yourself in the varied cultures along the Danube with performances that feature local folklore, traditional music, and dance. These cultural exhibitions look at the creative legacy of the areas you visit.

Live Music events: Indulge in live music events including genres like classical, jazz, or folk. Talented artists regularly adorn the aboard stages, offering a lovely backdrop to your vacation.

Interactive Performances: Some performances promote audience interaction, turning the performance into an immersive experience. Whether it's a dancing class or a comedy night, these participatory aspects generate unforgettable experiences.

Professional Performers: Cruise ships regularly include professional performers, ranging from magicians and comedians to dance troupes and solo musicians. These performers bring a high degree of expertise and creativity to the board stage.

Theatrical performances: Enjoy theatrical performances that may include themed plays, musicals, or even adaptations of local legends. These performances take you to other times and storylines, improving the cultural voyage.

Dinner Entertainment: Some cruises provide entertainment throughout dinner, upgrading your dining experience with live music, small ensembles, or private presentations that create a refined mood.

Onboard entertainment concerts are a dynamic component of your Danube River cruise, adding flare to your evenings and ensuring that every minute spent on the ship is filled with enchantment, cultural immersion, and the thrill of live performances.

Wine Tasting Sessions: A Sip of Culture and Terroir

Wine-tasting events aboard give a pleasant excursion through the vineyards that flank the Danube. Whether you're a seasoned oenophile or a casual appreciator of wine, these sessions give you a unique chance to taste the flavors of the locations you explore.

Typically hosted by skilled sommeliers or local experts, wine tastings dive into the intricacies of regional varietals, providing anecdotes of the vineyards and the winemaking process. Participants get to experience a range of wines, ranging from crisp whites to strong reds, each showcasing the terroir of the Danube Valley.

As you swirl, smell, and taste, you'll not only revel in the sensual pleasures of wine but also acquire insights into the cultural and historical importance of winemaking along the Danube. It's a social and educational experience, establishing a deeper connection with the locations you visit, one glass at a time.

Fitness Classes on Board: Energizing Your Danube Journey

Stay active and energized on your Danube River cruise with onboard fitness programs. These programs are intended to appeal to varied fitness levels, helping you maintain your well-being while enjoying the lovely surroundings along the river.

Key Features:

1. Guided exercises: Join professional fitness instructors for a selection of guided exercises, including aerobics, yoga, and strength training. These programs are geared to suit varied fitness levels, from beginners to more experienced athletes.

2. Scenic Exercise locations: Many river cruise ships have outdoor locations, such as sundecks, where fitness programs are done. Exercising against the background of the Danube's gorgeous surroundings provides an added element of pleasure to your exercise.

3. Wellness Programs: Some cruises feature holistic wellness programs, mixing exercise with mindfulness. Participate in activities like morning yoga or meditation classes to start your day with a renewed attitude.

4. Group Dynamics: Fitness sessions on board frequently promote a feeling of kinship among other tourists. Group workouts give a social and motivating factor, making it a pleasant and engaging experience.

5. Varied Class possibilities: Whether you prefer low-impact exercises like stretching or high-energy workouts, cruise fitness sessions often provide a range of possibilities. Choose courses that suit your exercise objectives and tastes.

6. Flexible Schedule: Cruise fitness programs normally feature flexible timetables, enabling you to engage at times that suit your daily agenda. Early morning yoga or an afternoon aerobics class—there's a choice for everyone.

Benefits:

- Health Integration: Fitness sessions complement the entire health experience of your voyage, harmonizing with the holistic approach many river cruise companies use.
- Stress Reduction: Exercise is a fantastic stress reliever. Amid the cultural adventures and touring, fitness sessions give a concentrated time for physical exertion and relaxation.

- Individual Attention: Instructors typically give individual attention, ensuring that participants maintain good technique and get the most out of their exercise.

Whether you're a keen fitness enthusiast or just want to add a little exercise to your cruise routine, onboard fitness courses provide a balanced and entertaining way to keep active while sailing the Danube.

Interactions with Locals

Engaging with people along the Danube is an enriching part of the river cruise experience, offering a true peek into the heart and soul of each town. Here's a peek at the different ways you may create meaningful ties with the people who call the Danube's beaches home:

1. Marketplace Banter:
- Wander through crowded local markets, where the brilliant tapestry of colors and fragrances sets the

backdrop for convivial discussions with merchants. Try your hand at a few local terms, and you could find yourself trading anecdotes about favorite area products.

2. Riverside Conversations:
- Stroll along the riverbanks and start-up talks with residents enjoying the environment. Whether it's a simple conversation with a fisherman casting their lines or a talk about the rich history of the area, these interactions give a true peek into everyday life.

3. Culinary Connections:
- Join a cooking lesson or eat in local businesses, where the warmth of welcome frequently goes beyond the plate. Conversations with chefs, restaurant owners, and other diners may give significant insights into culinary traditions and local tastes.

4. Folklore Performances:
- Attend local folklore performances, where traditional music and dance bring communities together. Don't hesitate to participate in the celebrations, whether it's a dance or just clapping along to the beat.

5. Artisan Workshops:
- Visit artisan workshops and connect with craftspeople who are maintaining old techniques. Learn about their crafts, ask questions, and maybe even try your hand at producing something unique to the area.

6. Cultural Events:

- Attend local events, festivals, or cultural gatherings where you may immerse yourself in the community atmosphere. Participate in rituals, watch performances, and join in the wonderful moments that mark local festivals.

7. Historical Narratives:
- When touring historical sites or museums, start-up talks with local guides or historians. Their tales typically go beyond facts and data, including human experiences that give a better knowledge of the region's past.

8. Language Exchange:
- Don't be hesitant about trying the local language. Even simple sentences express respect and openness, frequently motivating locals to react with a grin and a readiness to share their culture.

These contacts with residents along the Danube add to the depth of your trip experience, producing lasting memories that reach beyond the physical grandeur of the river and its environs. Whether via shared laughter, cultural insights, or meaningful interactions, these ties with locals constitute a vital aspect of the Danube's attraction.

Cruise Ship Accommodations

Cruise Ship Accommodations: Sailing in Comfort and Style

Cruise ship rooms along the Danube provide a choice of possibilities, assuring guests may choose a pleasant sanctuary tailored to their interests. Prices might vary depending on criteria such as stateroom type, cruise line, and particular amenities. Here's a peek at the lodging types you could encounter:

1. Inside Cabins:
- Price Range: $1,000 - $2,500
- These rooms, situated in the interior of the ship, provide pleasant quarters with all required conveniences. They give a budget-friendly choice for tourists who favor the cruise experience above vast in-cabin views.

2. Oceanview Cabins:
- Price Range: $1,500 - $3,500
- Oceanview accommodations have windows or portholes, enabling passengers to enjoy breathtaking views of the Danube right from their cabins. Prices vary depending on variables including cabin size and location.

3. Balcony Cabins:
- Prices Range: $2,500 - $5,000
- Balcony rooms feature private outside area, enabling visitors to relish the fresh air and spectacular views. The pricing range varies on criteria such as cruise line, stateroom size, and itinerary.

4. Suites:
- Price Range: $4,000 - $10,000+
- Suites provide larger lodgings with separate living spaces, additional facilities, and, in certain instances, special incentives. Prices vary greatly depending on the degree of luxury and cruise line.

5. Luxury Suites and Staterooms:
- Price Range: $8,000 - $20,000+
- For tourists wanting the greatest in luxury, cruise companies may provide top-tier suites with premium amenities, private butlers, and special privileges. The spectrum might expand depending on the amount of extravagance.

6. Single Cabins:
- Price Range: $1,500 - $4,000
- Cruise companies typically provide single rooms for lone guests, giving a pleasant and cost-effective choice. Prices might vary depending on the cruise company and the facilities offered.

7. Family Cabins:
- Price Range: $3,000 - $7,000

- Family cabins cater to bigger parties, providing interconnecting rooms or specialized family suites. Prices vary on the cruise company, cabin layout, and facilities given to families.

It's crucial to note that these pricing ranges might change depending on cruise company specials, the time of booking, and individual itineraries. Additionally, river cruises in the Danube may have different price dynamics compared to ocean cruises. Always verify with the cruise company for the most current and up-to-date price information depending on your choices and travel dates. Onshore Hotels & Lodgings

General overview of hotels along Danube

1. Luxury Hotels (Approx. $200 and more per night):
   - Hotel Sacher Vienna (Vienna, Austria): Located near the State Opera, this landmark hotel is recognized for its opulent suites and famed Sachertorte.

   - Four Seasons Hotel Gresham Palace (Budapest, Hungary): Situated along the Danube, this Art Nouveau jewel provides magnificent accommodations and spectacular views of the Chain Bridge.

2. Mid-Range Hotels (Approx. $100 - $200 per night):

- NH Collection Nürnberg City (Nuremberg, Germany): A contemporary hotel in the city of Nuremberg, providing comfort and convenience for mid-range budgets.

- Austria Trend Hotel Schloss Dürnstein (Dürnstein, Austria): Nestled in the Wachau Valley, this lovely hotel mixes history with modern conveniences.

3. Budget-Friendly Options (Below $100 per night):
- Hotel Gat Point Charlie (Bratislava, Slovakia): A budget-friendly hotel in the old city center, providing a pleasant stay without breaking the bank.

- Easyhotel Budapest Oktogon (Budapest, Hungary): An economical alternative in Budapest, providing simplicity and convenience for budget-conscious guests.

Chapter 10. Practical Travel Tips

Packing Essentials

Embarking on a Danube River cruise enables you to appreciate the splendor of European sites while floating down one of the continent's most renowned rivers. To guarantee a comfortable and pleasurable travel, consider bringing the following essentials:

1. Clothing:
- Casual Wear: Comfortable attire for daytime trips, including lightweight shirts, shorts, or skirts.
- Formal Attire: Pack a couple of semi-formal clothes for board meals or special occasions.
- Layers: Bring a light jacket or sweater for chilly nights, particularly if you're traveling in spring or autumn.
- Rain Gear: A waterproof jacket or travel umbrella might be helpful for unexpected rains.

2. Footwear:
- comfy Walking Shoes: Sneakers or comfy walking shoes are necessary for touring cobblestone streets and historical places.
- Dress Shoes: Include a pair of dressier shoes for formal nights or dining aboard.

3. Accessories:

- Sun Protection: Sunglasses, a wide-brimmed hat, and sunscreen to defend oneself from the European sun while onshore activities.
- Daypack: A tiny daypack is ideal for transporting necessities on outings.
- Travel Adapters: Ensure you have the necessary power adapters for the countries you'll be traveling to charge your gadgets.

4. Travel Documents:
- Passport and Visa: Ensure your passport is valid for at least six months beyond your scheduled trip. Check visa requirements for the countries you'll travel to.
- Travel Insurance: Carry documentation of your travel insurance policy.
- Cruise Documents: Include your cruise itinerary, tickets, and any relevant reservation confirmations.

5. Health and Medications:
- Prescription Medications: Pack enough for the length of your vacation, along with a copy of your prescription.
- Basic First Aid Kit: Include necessities like painkillers, bandages, and any personal meds.

6. Technology and Entertainment:
- Camera: Capture the breathtaking splendor along the Danube. Don't forget additional memory cards and charging supplies.
- E-Reader or Books: Enjoy some reading during downtime.

- Adapter and Chargers: Bring chargers for your gadgets and confirm they are compatible with European outlets.

7. Toiletries:
- Travel-Sized Toiletries: Pack travel-sized shampoo, conditioner, toothbrush, and other personal care goods.
- Wet Wipes or Hand Sanitizer: Useful for fast cleanups on trips.

8. Money and Security:
- Credit Cards and Cash: Notify your bank of your trip dates and pack some local money for little transactions.
- Money Belt or Neck bag: Consider utilizing a safe bag to keep valuables handy on outings.

9. Miscellaneous:
- Travel Pillow: Handy for comfort during lengthy travels or resting on the ship.
- Reusable Water Bottle: Stay hydrated throughout trips.
- Collapsible Tote Bag: Ideal for transporting souvenirs or other goods obtained on your trip.

10. Snorkeling Gear (for certain itineraries):
- If your cruise includes stops at places suited for snorkeling, pack your snorkel, mask, and fins.

Remember to adapt your packing list depending on the unique season, activities, and places included in your Danube River cruise itinerary. Additionally, check with your cruise company for any special dress standards or suggested goods depending on their services and activities.

Language Tips and Common Phrases Across Danube Destinations

Embracing the local languages along the Danube adds a lovely depth to your cultural experience. While English is typically spoken in tourist regions, making an effort to speak in the local tongue may establish bonds. Here are some linguistic hints and common words across numerous Danube destinations:

1. German (Austria, Germany):
- Hello: Hallo
- Thank you: Danke
- Goodbye: Auf Wiedersehen
- Excuse me: Entschuldigung
- Yes/No: Ja/Nein

2. Hungarian (Hungary):
- Hello: Szia (casual), Jó napot (formal)
- Thank you: Köszönöm
- Goodbye: Viszlát
- Excuse me: Elnézést
- Yes/No: Igen/Nem

3. Slovak (Slovakia):

- Hello: Ahoj
- Thank you: Ďakujem
- Goodbye: Dovidenia
- Excuse me: Prepáčte
- Yes/No: Áno/Nie

4. Serbian (Serbia):
- Hello: Zdravo
- Thank you: Hvala
- Goodbye: Doviđenja
- Excuse me: Izvinite
- Yes/No: Da/Ne

5. Romanian (Romania):
- Hello: Buna ziua
- Thank you: Mulţumesc
- Goodbye: La revere
- Excuse me: Scuzaţi-mă
- Yes/No: Da/Nu

6. Bulgarian (Bulgaria):
- Hello: Здравейте (Zdraveyte)
- Thank you: Благодаря (Blagodarya)
- Goodbye: Довиждане (Dovizhdane)
- Excuse me: Извинете (Izvinete)
- Yes/No: Да/Не (Da/Ne)

7. Croatian (Croatia):
- Hello: Bok
- Thank you: Hvala
- Goodbye: Doviđenja

- Excuse me: Oprostite
- Yes/No: Da/Ne

8. Czech (Czech Republic):
- Hello: Ahoj
- Thank you: Děkuji
- Goodbye: Na shledanou
- Excuse me: Promiňte
- Yes/No: Ano/Ne

Language Tips:
- Greet with a grin: A warm grin is widely recognized and appreciated.
- Learn Basic Numbers: Especially important for transactions and directions.
- Use Polite Phrases: "Please" and "thank you" go a long way in any language.
- Practice Pronunciation: Locals will generally appreciate your efforts even if the pronunciation isn't flawless.

Remember, attempting to learn the local language, no matter how elementary, shows respect and frequently leads to more meaningful encounters on your Danube River cruise.

Currency Tips and Local Currencies Along the Danube River.

Navigating the varied places along the Danube River means experiencing several currencies. Here are monetary advice and an overview of local currencies across several significant destinations:

1. Euro (€):
- Used in Austria, Slovakia, and Germany.
- Currency Tips: Euros are generally accepted, and you may withdraw them from ATMs in these nations. Inform your bank of your trip dates to prevent any complications with card transactions.

2. Hungarian Forint (HUF):
- Used in Hungary.
- money Tips: Exchange some money before arrival or withdraw Hungarian Forints from local ATMs. Major credit cards are typically accepted, although bringing cash to smaller places is essential.

3. Czech Koruna (CZK):
- Used in the Czech Republic.
- Currency Tips: Currency exchange bureaus are prominent in tourist regions. Credit cards are frequently accepted, however, carrying some local cash for minor transactions is important.

4. Croatian Kuna (HRK):
- Used in Croatia (if visiting locations along the Danube in Croatia).
- currencies Tips: Exchange currencies at banks or currency exchange bureaus. Credit cards are accepted in

bigger places, however cash may be preferred in smaller areas.

5. Serbian Dinar (RSD):
- Used in Serbia.
- Currency Tips: Exchange currency at local banks or exchange bureaus. Credit cards are accepted in metropolitan regions, but carrying cash is vital in rural settings.

6. Bulgarian Lev (BGN):
- Used in Bulgaria.
- Currency Tips: Exchange currencies at banks or currency exchange bureaus. Credit cards are frequently accepted in bigger cities, although cash may be preferred in smaller towns and rural regions.

7. Romanian Leu (RON):
- Used in Romania.
- Currency Tips: Exchange currencies at banks or exchange bureaus. Credit cards are frequently accepted in metropolitan areas, although cash is advised for rural sites.

8. Euro (€) - Again:
- Used in: Slovakia and Germany.
- Currency Tips: Similar to Austria, Euros are commonly accepted in Slovakia and Germany. ATMs are accessible for withdrawals in local currency.

General Currency Tips:

- Currency Exchange Locations: Use official exchange offices or banks for currency exchange to guarantee fair prices.
- ATM Withdrawals: ATMs are typically present in metropolitan areas. Inform your bank about your trip dates to prevent any complications with card transactions.

- tiny Denominations: Keep tiny denominations for gratuities, local markets, and modest purchases. Larger banknotes may not be accepted everywhere.

- Check Currency Symbols: Be mindful of currency symbols to minimize misunderstanding, particularly when employing multiple currencies nearby.

Remember that currency use might differ among nations, and it's smart to carry a mix of cash and cards.

Useful Resources

Photography Tips To Enhance Your Adventure

For Both Smartphone and Digital Camera Users:

1. Golden Hour Magic:
- Leverage the soft, warm light during the golden hours (early morning or late afternoon) for lovely sceneries.

This lighting accentuates the colors and gives a wonderful touch to your images.

2. Focus on Composition:
- Apply fundamental composition concepts like the rule of thirds. Place major objects like the river, bridges, or castles along these lines to create visually attractive pictures.

3. Capture Reflections:
- Utilize the shiny surface of the Danube to catch spectacular reflections. Calm seas early in the morning or around dusk give great circumstances.

4. Experiment with Angles:
- Play with various perspectives to provide a new perspective to familiar situations. Capture low-angle pictures for a unique perspective of the riverbanks and architecture.

5. Include Foreground Elements:
- Incorporate fascinating foreground items to provide depth and dimension to your images. This might be river pebbles, flowers, or architectural elements.

6. Zoom with Your Feet:
- Instead of depending exclusively on digital zoom, physically walk closer to your topic. This preserves picture quality and produces crisper photographs.

7. Use HDR Mode:

- High Dynamic Range (HDR) setting helps balance exposure in adverse lighting situations. It's especially beneficial for capturing landscapes with brilliant sky and dark sections.

For Smartphone Users:

8. Tap to Focus and Adjust Exposure:
- Take control of your smartphone's camera by touching on the screen to select focus and exposure. This ensures the primary subject is crisp, and exposure is well-balanced.

9. Utilize Panorama Mode:
- Capture the immensity of the Danube by utilizing your smartphone's panoramic function. Slowly pan over the subject for wide landscape photos.

10. Experiment with Camera Apps:
- Explore third-party camera applications that give manual controls. This lets you alter parameters like ISO and shutter speed for greater creative flexibility.

For Digital Camera Users:

11. Shoot in RAW Format:
- If your camera supports it, shoot in RAW format. This allows you greater versatility in post-processing, enabling you to improve details and colors.

12. Manual Mode for Control:

- Experiment with manual settings to alter the aperture, shutter speed, and ISO. This is very important when dealing with tough lighting circumstances.

13. Carry a Tripod:
- For low-light circumstances or long-exposure photographs, a tiny portable tripod helps steady your camera and avoid fuzzy images.

Remember, the most essential component of photography is to have fun and capture the moments that connect with you. Experiment with these methods and get your viewpoint on the lovely vistas along the Danube.

Websites and Useful Contacts

Here are some valuable websites and links that might improve your Danube River cruise experience:

1. Cruise Lines:
- [Viking River Cruises](https://www.vikingrivercruises.com/)
- [AmaWaterways](https://www.amawaterways.com/)
- [Uniworld Boutique River Cruises](https://www.uniworld.com/)
- [Avalon Waterways](https://www.avalonwaterways.com/)
- [Emerald Waterways](https://www.emeraldwaterways.com/)

2. Currency Exchange & Conversion:
- [XE Currency Converter](https://www.xe.com/currencyconverter/)
- [OANDA Currency Converter](https://www.oanda.com/currency/converter/)

3. Local Tourism Boards:
- [Austria Tourism Board](https://www.austria.info/)
- [Hungary Tourism Board](https://visithungary.com/)
- [Germany National Tourist Board](https://www.germany.travel/en)
- [Slovakia Tourism Board](https://slovakia.travel/en)
- [Serbia Tourist Organization](http://www.serbia.travel/)
- [Bulgaria Tourism](https://bulgariatravel.org/en/)
- [Romania Tourism](http://romaniatourism.com/)

4. Language Learning Apps:
- [Duolingo](https://www.duolingo.com/)
- [Babbel](https://www.babbel.com/)
- [Memrise](https://www.memrise.com/)

5. Health and Safety:
- [CDC - Travel Health Notices](https://wwwnc.cdc.gov/travel/notices)
- [World Health Organization (WHO)](https://www.who.int/)

6. Local Emergency Contacts:
- Emergency services: 112 (universal emergency number in the European Union)
- Local emergency numbers may vary by country, so educate yourself with the precise numbers for each visit.

7. Weather Forecasts:
- [BBC Weather - Danube Region](https://www.bbc.com/weather)

8. Transportation:
- [Eurolines - International Bus Service](https://www.eurolines.com/)
- [Eurail - European Train Travel](https://www.eurail.com/)

9. Local Events and Festivals:
- Check local tourist websites for information on events and festivals occurring during your stay.

Always verify and review the newest information before your trip, and feel free to seek other resources depending on your unique interests and requirements. Safe travels!

Made in the USA
Monee, IL
23 January 2024

52256849R00075